D0857353

Pry

PROGRESS OR DISASTER?

From the Bourgeois to the World Citizen

PROGRESS OR DISASTER?

From the Bourgeois to the World Citizen

ROBERT ULICH

Harvard University

New York · New York University Press
London · University of London Press Ltd

1971

The day is short, and the work is great, and the laborers are sluggish . . . and the Master is urgent. . . . It is not thy duty to complete the work, but neither art thou free to desist from it.

Sayings of the Jewish Fathers

There is one thing stronger than all the armies of the earth, and that is an idea whose time has come.

Victor Hugo

PREFACE

If one asked me how long I have been working on this book, I could answer: "Five years spent in concentrated writing, and a whole adult life spent in the attempt to extract some meaning from the experiences and observations in various countries and fields of action." Although I never speak of myself *directly*, this book is, in a way, autobiographical. There is little in it that I do not remember personally as the result of intense participation in the period of deceptive security before World War I, the collapse of the old order during the two international wars, and finally, the perplexities of our immediate present. Are we going from one catastrophe to another, or are we in a period of painful transmission to a new civilization—and of what kind?

A society, just as an individual person, can mature only if it has no illusions about the dark powers that lurk in the recesses of men's souls. But it must also have trust in the potentials and the will power that can lift humanity above itself. We must be aware of both if we want to be makers of history and not its victims.

Like an increasing number of people, I believe that there is one vision that could help us turn danger into challenge and confusion into constructive purpose: the unity of mankind. Actually, this idea is as old as man's great philosophical and religious speculations. But hitherto it has been buried in the drab grounds of self-assertion, aggressiveness, and sheer stupidity.

Either the period of moral and military conflicts has taught us that mankind will ruin itself if it continues on the path of the past, or the unspeakable suffering we have gone through has rendered us sufficiently mature for the great step forward from nationalist separation toward international cooperation.

This book is an attempt to prove that the cultural changes characteristic of the past two centuries can be described as widening circles from narrow to broad relations between nations and races. Let us hope for statesmen and educators who, supported by an intelligent and vigilant citizenry, listen to what history tries to tell us—that the ever increasing spatial proximity and interdependence of men can turn into disaster without adequate moral preparation but into a blessing if we try to understand and help each other.

One never knows all the deeper motivations that cause an author to write a book. But for me, one of them came from my long work in the Council on the Study of Mankind, with the founder of which, Gerhard Hirschfeld, I had many conferences and a continuous correspondence. I also look gratefully back at the hospitality of Dr. Edmund and Margiana Stinnes at one of the loveliest places in Europe, the Casa Signor in Croce on the hills of Ascona, and the hospitality of Professor Frederick Ellis, Western Washington State College, and his wife Marilyn at another beautiful location, Shaw Island, one of the San Juan Islands which decorate the coast of the Pacific near the Canadian-American border. In one way or another, they all have helped me to collect and compose my ideas. But I would accuse myself of a lack of gratefulness if I did not especially remember the infinite patience of Frederick Ellis when he discussed with me, his former teacher at Harvard, the issues dealt with in this book as well as the intricacies of the English language. Invariably this discussion extended from merely linguistic into general human problems, for language is not merely a mode of communication. It is also a mirror of the culture of the people who speak it, and it is ultimately a mirror of man.

I am also indebted to my colleague, Professor Israel Scheffler of Harvard, for reading and commenting upon the manuscript.

CONTENTS

Part I. The Era of Bourgeois-Imperialism

Introduction   3

Criteria for judging a historical period. The term
"bourgeois." Characteristics of bourgeois culture. Matthew
Arnold's distinction between the Barbarians, the Philistines, and the Populace.

1. *The State and the Economy*   9

   1. The State

   The myth and reality of the state. The ancients. Thomas
   Aquinas. The Enlightenment. Hegel. Herbert Spencer.
   Liberalism. The idea of Progress. Marx's criticism and the
   threat of international socialism.

   2. The Economy

   Industrial capitalism and its influence on the value
   system of the bourgeois. The profit motive and the concept of efficiency. The exploitation of the workers. Industrial imperialism. Colonialism.

2. *Religion, Humanism, and Education*   27

1. Religion

Religion as convention. Critics of Christian super-naturalism: Ernest Renan, David Friedrich Strauss, Ernst Haeckel. New concepts of man's destiny: Kierkegaard, Nietzsche, Freud. Failure to disturb the self-confidence of the bourgeois. The prophecy of Heinrich Heine.

2. Humanism

The shift from world-transcendence to world-immanence. Renaissance, Montaigne, Goethe, Spencer, William James. Spinoza's concept of *Libertas philosophandi*. Freedom. Tolerance. Contradictions and overlapping attitudes. Humanitarianism and application of humanist ideas to social problems.

3. Education

Class structure. Rise of popular education as a means of national conformity. Education as a means of national competition. Demand for better education on the part of the workers. Rise of anarchism, humanitarian motives. Highly selective standards in advanced forms of education. Predominance of the classics. Emerging criticism. *Humanitas* and the gentleman ideal.

4. Evaluation

One-sidedness of the typical criticism of the bourgeois. Achievements. Lack of authenticity and self-identity in the mentality of the bourgeois. Catastrophical influence of militarism and national rivalries leading to World War I.

Part II. The Years of Catastrophe

3. *The State and the Economy* 51

1. The State

Long period of relative peace during the bourgeois era explains the sense of security in spite of mounting tension and armament. Abortive attempts by liberal and socialist groups to avoid war.

End of the period of the bourgeois. Collapse of the monarchical order in Austria, Germany, and Russia. The slogan "To make the world safe for democracy." Lack of democratic experience in the defeated nations. Disillusionment in Woodrow Wilson's "Fourteen Points." Dishonesty of international politics and the breakdown of the League of Nations. The myopic attitude of the victors. The rise of totalitarianism. The "Red Terror" and the victory of communism in Russia.

2. The Economy

Increasing importance of central governments. The inflation and its psychological effects. Collapse of business. Depression, despair, and the National-Socialist experiment.

4. *Religion, Humanism, and Education* 60

1. Religion

Failure of the Churches and defeat of moral standards by the war spirit. Confusing effects of the Concordat of Pius XII with Hitler and "the capitulation of German Catholicism." The attitude of Protestantism.

Reasons for adjustment of the Catholic and other Churches to dictatorial governments. The political consequences of the principles of obedience and authority in

Catholic education. Church diplomacy vs. the courage of Christian testimony.

2. Humanism

Shattered confidence in man. Return to supernaturalism. Agnosticism and cynicism. In the United States the prevailing philosophies of pragmatism and experimentalism (John Dewey) appear inadequate to the problems of man in a situation of crisis. "Philosophies of Life" in Europe, that is, Wilhelm Dilthey and Henri Bergson. Vanishing influence of the older idealistic systems without new directing ideas. Kierkegaard's Christian subjectivism, Nietzsche's atheism and Freud's psychoanalysis as signs of a radically new interpretation of man. Rise of the existentialist movement as protest against preconceived philosophical premises: Jaspers, Heidegger. Parallels to philosophical existentialism in belles lettres: Kafka, Camus, Sartre. The nakednes of man. Distortion of the fullness of human existence in existentialism.

3. Education

Educational "progressivism" as reaction to the failure of Western civilization. Activist conception of the "educational process." Dewey's "learning by doing" and Pestalozzi's "organic education." The "child-centered" school. The merits of progressive education. Lack of experience and of total comprehension of human culture on the part of many reformers. The purposefulnes of education in the USSR.

Part III.   The Postwar Era and the Dawn of the Idea of Mankind

5. *The State and the Economy*   85

1. The State

Increasing necessity of international cooperation in an era of mutual global interdependence. Nevertheless heightened nationalism as result of increasing dependence of the citizen on the state.

The new tasks of world leaders. 1) Reconciliation of patriotic loyalty with international commitment. 2) Rational thinking concerning co-existence of democracy and communism. 3) Balance between political consensus and the right of dissension. 4) Solution of the racial problem. 5) Birth control.

Doubt concerning democracy in the United States and mellowing of the revolutionary spirit in Soviet Russia. Possibilities of convergence between different political systems. Fundamental differences.

2. The Economy

I. The Inseparability of Economics and Politics. The power of big corporations. Limitation of their power through legislation. Government spending in the international field: Lend-Lease Plan, Marshall Plan, Foreign Aid Programs. Short-sighted opposition to international financing. Disparity in the economic resources between the northern and southern hemispheres.

II. Capitalism versus Communism (The inadequacy of our traditional political vocabulary. Class structure and elitism also in the Soviet countries. Increasing influence of the workers in capitalist enterprise. "Capitalist" or "cooperative" democracy? Necessity and danger of the welfare state. Gradual collectivization of life and mind.)

III. Specific Features of the Postwar Era (Artificiality

and vulnerability of modern civilization. Obsession with speed. Changes in the structure of business itself.) (1) The Individual Enterpreneur versus the Corporation (2) Planning and Group Decision (3) Advertising and Communication (4) The "New Estate" and the Education of the Businessman.

6. *Religion, Humanism, and Education*   127

1. Religion

Contrasting opinions with regard to the role of religion in our time. Influence of the World Wars on the religious conscience. Incompatibility between Christian dogma and modern knowledge. Dilemma of the clergy.

I. The Protestant Situation (Attempts to separate superstitious from essential elements in the Christian tradition. Lack of logical clarity. The "death of God" theologians. Protestantism a sinking ship or *ecclesia semper reformanda.*)

II. The Catholic Situation (Pope John XXIII. The "aggiornamento" or the Ecumenical Council (Vaticanum II) Ambiguities in the reform movement. Challenge to Catholic conscience. *Humanae Vitae* (Birth control) and the Dutch Catechism. Unrest in the Catholic clergy and wavering of the essentially conservative Pope Paul VI. Growing demand for participation among laymen. Disintegration and survival.)

2. Humanism.

I. The Relation to the Past
II. The Relation to Religion
III. Humanism and Optimism
IV. Humanist Optimism
V. Humanist Ethics

3. Education

Transition from regional to universal attitudes. Obstacles. Dogmatic world views. The psychology of nationalism. The rebellion of youth. The Teacher and controversial topics. The cultivation of creativity and the characteristics of the creative person: spontaneity, sensitivity, self-discipline, purposefulness, imagination, truthfulness, involvement. Creativity and mass education. Lack of philosophical design in modern education. Its antibiological quality. The professorial empire. Necessity of radical reform. The invincibility of learning as the hope for a new consciousness for mankind.

Epilogue 188

1. Politics and the Economy

The new world. Soviet Russia, the United States and China replace the old monarchies. Interdependence threatened by nationalism in many parts of the world.

Wealth versus poverty. Contrast between developed and developing nations.

2. Religion and Humanism

Religious modernism and religious obscurantism. The desire for belonging.

3. Education

The environment of the coming generations and the tasks of the schools. Ignorance about basic educational problems. Necessity of radical reorganization and its obstacles. The parents. The perennial power of education and the idea of mankind.

Index 204

Part I

The Era of Bourgeois Imperialism

INTRODUCTION

Each historical period will ultimately be judged according to one criterion: what has it contributed to mankind? Mankind in its entirety will be the judge. It will ask not only to what degree individual persons and nations have excelled others in politics, thought, science, and the arts. It will also ask to what degree these achievements have brought the multitudes of men closer to each other and instilled in them convictions of more universal validity, or truth, than those of limited origin and intention.

What this truth is no one can describe exactly. It is both intellectual and moral. And it certainly is not consensus; that would be the triumph of mediocrity. Yet every sensitive person knows of the challenging presence of the ideal even though he is still far away from it, struggling, striving, despairing, and nevertheless aware that he would give up himself if he gave up fighting. For with every step forward he feels uplifted, freer, and closer to the abiding—whatever it is. And he wishes the same for other people and peoples.

It is the purpose of this book to inquire how the era in which we live—roughly delimited here to the nineteenth and twentieth centuries—will be judged by later generations. What have we contributed to the gradual self-realization of mankind? To phrase it more precisely, are we, by virtue of our intellectual and technical achievements, gradually approaching a higher and more universal state of civilization than our ancestors, or—great managers and engineers though undoubtedly we are—are we preparing the ultimate victory of organized mass barbarism and mass murder?

Certainly, no enterprise is more exposed to the making of dubious generalizations than that of judging a whole historical period, for every period is but a concourse of contradictory tendencies and transitions from one fleeting point of time to another. Who can say exactly when and where the journey of our modern civilization began and where it will end? The Greeks, the Romans, the medieval saints, and the genius of the Renaissance are still with us, transfigured, of course, but somehow alive. And so are their mistakes, their crimes, and their wars. Nevertheless, we are aware of certain dominant trends that have rendered our period different from earlier ones.

We no longer live under the authority of the Church and the social and intellectual norms of feudal absolutism. They were challenged by the cooperation of science and the Enlightenment of the eighteenth century. The liberal revolutions of 1789, 1830, and 1848 forced monarchism to yield to republicanism or at least to some compromise with it. At the same time, the machine took over the work of the hand and changed the life and the environment of man more rapidly than had ever happened in human history. The past two hundred years possessed and bequeathed to us an amazing capacity for drawing into their vortex the most varied trends of the past. But, like every historical phase that does not end in stagnation, this era has also been the seedbed of forces that have finally destroyed many of the beliefs under the guidance of which the era began. This is especially true of religion.

The first of the three periods under consideration—that before World War I—I will call the period of the bourgeois. As a political figure with which the older classes had to reckon, the bourgeois emerged at the end of the eighteenth century although the bourgeois appeared during the sixteenth and seventeenth centuries, when the Protestant Reformation and the Thirty Years' War destroyed the medieval order. The bourgeois is still with us, but he is no longer certain of himself and is no longer such a determining force in the determination of the political and cultural climate of the leading nations as he was during the nineteenth century. World War I brought with it the first great disappointment. Since then, calamities have piled up with every new decade.

The term "bourgeois," as used here, will refer not only to the wealthy members of industry and finance but also to the comfortable, though not rich, middle of the middle classes, the petit bourgeois. Every year he put aside a sum of money gained from his plant or his wholesale business in order to retire when he felt he had had enough and to leave the enterprise to one of his sons. The other sons went perhaps into the professions, and his daughters received a nice dowry so that the sons-in-law did not need to pay for the furniture and linens of the new households. Even the petit bourgeois' style of living and thinking could be easily distinguished from that of the farmer and the landowning aristocracy on the one side, and, on the other, from that of the so-called lower middle classes, whose occupations were typically those of clerks, subordinate officials with low income, artisans, or store owners. They all, of course, looked with a mixture of superiority and apprehensiveness to the "fourth estate," that amorphous mass of the proletariat, as described by Marx in his *Das Kapital.*

In the older sociological literature, Matthew Arnold's classification of the English society enjoyed much popularity because this classification, though somewhat fanciful, applies not only to Britain but also to the other industrial societies of his era.

In Arnold's *Culture and Anarchy* [1] (1869), he distinguishes between the "Barbarians," the "Philistines," and the "Populace." To the Barbarians belongs the aristocrat, who takes care of his body; likes sports; and possesses courage, self-confidence, choice manners, and distinguished bearing. The culture of the aristocracy is "exterior chiefly." It suffers from an insufficiency of depth, and even in its feminine half, "there should perhaps, for ideal perfection, be a shade more *soul.*"

In contradistinction, the Philistines of the industrial middle class represent the spirit of enterprise. Indeed, in spite of the number of aristocrats still found in parliament, official positions

1. *Culture and Anarchy, An Essay in Politics and Social Criticism* (New York: Macmillan, 1897; first edition, 1869), pp. 77ff.

and government, the Philistines "have done all the great things that have been done in all departments." They are the real leaders of modern society. They are "stiffnecked" and prefer "to sweetness and light . . . that sort of machinery of business, chapels, tea-meetings, and addresses from Mr. Murphy, which makes up the dismal and illiberal life [of business] on which I have so often touched." Particularly notorious among the Philistines are new commercial members of Parliament and their opposites, the fanatical Protestant dissenters.

Finally, there is the Populace. The populace has built the railroads, made the goods, and transported the cargoes of "the greatest mercantile navy the world has ever seen." This part of the Populace—so Mr. Arnold predicts—"is, or is in a fair way to be, one in spirit with the industrial middle class." Indeed, the liberals already look forward to a´ unity of labor and the Philistines "because it is its class and its class instinct which it seeks to affirm—its ordinary self; and it is a machinery, an industrial machinery, and power and pre-eminence and other external goods, which fills its thoughts, and not an inward perfection."

But, so Mr. Arnold writes in his rambling manner, "All of us, so far as we are Barbarians, Philistines, or Populace, imagine happiness to consist in doing what one's ordinary self likes. What one's ordinary self likes differs according to the class to which one belongs, and has its severe and its lighter side; always, however, remaining machinery and nothing more."

Much of this Arnoldian venture is one-sided, and, as far as the Philistines are concerned, is derived largely from the nonconformist and anti-Anglican spirit of the English business class. In view of the actual material and educational situation of the workers, especially among the English, his prediction of the consummation of the populace into the ranks of the Philistines is highly premature. He himself speaks of the poverty and squalor in which the working class "raw and half-developed, has long lain half-hidden." But Mr. Arnold clearly observes the effect on this class of its trade unions and other political activities. Labor "is now issuing from its hiding place to assert an Englishman's heaven-born privilege of doing as he likes, and is beginning to perplex us by marching where it likes, meeting where it likes, bawling what it likes, breaking what it likes."

Thus, when one abstracts the specific English peculiarities from Mr. Arnold's picture, it contains not only much that is generally true of the society of the bourgeois in the second half of the nineteenth century but also some prophetic vision about the mingling of the social classes in modern society.

Just as the bourgeois modernized the old social order, so he modernized the cities. He broke down their walls and gates, destroyed dignified houses in order to construct ugly post offices and still uglier factories, and recklessly led the tracks of railways through romantic old streets and gardens into the center of towns. The modern slum crept insidiously from the docks and warehouses toward former parks and avenues where the respectable citizen liked to take his evening stroll. The nice old pub changed into the saloon, and the fight began between gangs and the police. The soul of humanity protested, but few listened, for some price had to be paid for the inevitable "march of progress."

Often the artist, particularly the novelist, has been the finest interpreter of human society. Thus the spirit of the bourgeois, good and bad, has found its most astute expositors in Charles Dickens, Honoré de Balzac, Anatole France, Gustave Flaubert, Emile Zola, Henry James, John Galsworthy, and Thomas Mann. And since Alexis de Tocqueville's *De la démocratie en Amérique* is as much the work of a great and intuitive artist as it is a historical masterpiece, he should also be mentioned.

As with all advanced civilizations of some form and endurance, society before World War I received its measure of unity from five interrelated powers: the state, guaranteeing the proper relation between man and the civil order; the economic system, concerned with the provision and proper distribution of the material means of man's existence; religion, interpreting the life of man in its dependence on higher powers; humanism, trying to explain man as a natural being and nature as governed by cosmic laws; and finally education, as the process of transmission and modification of values from one generation to the next.

These five basic elements of civilized societies never function to man's complete satisfaction. Perhaps ancient Egypt and the Byzantine Empire, with a divine monarch and a stern hierarchy of priests and officials, or Tibet before the Chinese conquest, achieved for some time a degree of unquestioned order. But modern man would suffocate in societies of conformity and collective submission to supposedly divine authorities. Since the era of the bourgeois began, he has felt the challenge of freedom, with all its risks and all its possibilities.

Chapter 1

THE STATE AND THE ECONOMY

1. THE STATE

With few exceptions, before World War I the bourgeois was a good, even a fervent patriot who believed the nation-state to be the strongest pillar of civilization, the apogee of historical evolution. It protected the life and right of the citizen against inner and outer enemies; it had become a strong partner in the economic system; and whether directly or indirectly, it was involved in many of the cultural and educational activities of the people.

The nation-state derived its influence and prestige from several sources. One of them reached into myth. In the universities the professors told their students that since ancient times the institution of the state (the right and just state) had been glorified as a reflection of cosmic unity or of the divine order that permeates all life. Such had been the belief of the pre-Socratic philosopher Heraclitus of the sixth century B.C. and his contemporary, Confucius, and of Plato, Aristotle, and the Romans. Thomas Aquinas, the Catholic canonical philosopher, elevated the Christian church above all earthly government; according to him, it had been appointed by Christ as the mediator between God and the human soul. Nevertheless, he explained the nature of human law and of its protector, the state, in a fashion essentially similar to that of the ancients. Divine law, so he taught, was embodied in the laws of rational creatures living in organized communities. As the medieval structure was shaken by ecclesiastical divisions and civil and international wars, many Catholic, Protestant, and secular thinkers discussed the role of the state more critically, especially since one could hardly contemplate the function of governments and nations without the crucial issue of war and peace. Francisco Suárez, Hugo Grotius, Thomas Hobbes, John Locke, and others developed the modern philosophy of government and international law, which, in contrast to other branches of philosophy, remained not merely in the realm of theory but urged a degree of decency on the leaders of nations and their armies, such as the protection of civilians, war prisoners, and the merchant mariners. Unfortunately, World War I marked the beginning of a new era of ruthless violence and engulfed the victors as well as the defeated in the chaos of the previous five years.

From whatever angle one approaches the problems of state and government, no one will deny that they reach deeply into the center of man's existence. For it depends on the civil order whether his rights as a human being are preserved or destroyed, whether he can live in the house of civilization or is condemned to stand before its doors, whether his children are taught to read and write or have to live in ignorance and poverty.

Generally, the German philosopher Friedrich Wilhelm Hegel is considered to have been the most influential glorifier of the state. The state appears to him as the guarantor of human values, as the instrument without which mankind could never achieve its highest goal: the appearance of universal Reason and Freedom, expressing themselves in the forms of religion, philosophy, and art. Hegel was by no means a nationalist reactionary, as some writers suppose who never read his original work.[1] Rather, he was one of the few who acknowledged the necessity of the French Revolution even in its failure. But he also admired those nations and their governments which in the midst of international chaos had been able to preserve some civil and international order—Austria, England, Prussia, and

1. The widely used translation of Hegel's *Philosophie der Geschichte* by J. Sibree, *The Philosophy of History* (New York: The Colonial Press, 1900; last edition), is so defective that it is difficult to identify parts of it (especially pp. 37ff.) with the original text. See instead: *The Philosophy of Hegel.* Edited, with an introduction, by Carl J. Friedrich (New York: Modern Library, 1953.)

Russia—which, of course, the military nobility and the prosperous middle classes liked to hear.

Hegel's philosophy contains mythological, conservative, romantic, and evolutionary elements, all overarched by a grand metaphysical system. This is the reason why he appealed to the most motley group of followers: reactionaries, theologians, liberals, and Socialists. They all could make themselves believe that the "World Mind" which secretly directed the course of history was on their side.

Hegel's philosophy blends happily with the rationalist traditions of the Enlightenment and its faith in progress. The Englishmen Locke and Hume and the Frenchmen Montesquieu and Diderot had advised their contemporaries to use the gift of reason to courageously take their future into their own hands rather than to obey passively those who happened to be their political and ecclesiastical superiors. For his own and his community's welfare, man should use science, empirical methods, and the ethics of well-understood self-interest. Henceforth the bourgeois, in contrast to the defenders of feudalism and ecclesiasticism, no longer regarded his state as an immutable product of divine dispensation, with princes on the top and people at the bottom, but as an institution that allowed him to change the hitherto stagnating human society into a community of enterprising citizens. "Progress," wrote Herbert Spencer in his *Social Statics*,[2] is not an accident but a necessity. Instead of civilization being artificial, it is a part of nature; all of a piece with the development of the embryo or the unfolding of a flower . . . as surely as there is any efficacy in educational culture, or any meaning in such terms as habit, custom and practice;—so surely must the human faculties be moulded into complete fitness for the social state; so surely must the things we call evil and immorality disappear; so surely must man become perfect."

Whereas Hegel, the brooding German metaphysician, conceived of progress as the result of the struggle between opposing forces under the guidance of the World Mind, Spencer, the Englishman, was so enchanted by the technical and scientific

2. *Social Statics, or The Conditions Essential to Human Happiness* (London, 1851), p. 65.

advances of his time that his proclaimed empiricism became a sort of utopianism. Hegel's insight into the conflictful nature of life explains why in all Western countries he attracted the attention of thinking men, whereas Spencer was almost forgotten until today, when his sociological acumen has begun to receive new appreciation.

Of course, many bourgeois, especially in the pious English middle classes, did not share Spencer's blooming optimism, especially for religious reasons. For although the Christian dogma of the natural depravity of man was gradually yielding to a more benign opinion about his moral chances, many still believed in original sin and in the salvation of man through Jesus Christ alone.

Nevertheless, besides the mythological-metaphysical and the rationalist-progressive ideas (both, paradoxically enough, culminating in Hegel), a third element had already crept into the attitude toward life, society, and the state of the active middle classes. Although they might have repudiated Spencer's secularism, they believed that change was the result of man's power of initiative and adaptation. Reactionary kings had been decapitated; empires had fallen; even wealth did not last. The only thing that worked was work, initiative, and the willingness to change. Otherwise: "From slave to slave in three generations."

Was not the national state itself a shining illustration of the stern laws of the survival of the fittest? From the fifteenth to the seventeenth centuries, absolutist monarchs had transformed the disintegrating feudalism of the Middle Ages into an efficient political system. With their big guns they had leveled the castles of rebellious vassals. In France they had united the nobility and the people of Normandy, Brittany, and Auvergne; in England they had made loyal Englishmen out of the inhabitants of Lancaster, Wales, and York; whereas in Germany and Italy—divided into dozens of small and jealous principalities—nationhood had to wait until the latter part of the nineteenth century. Particularism, political and religious, still threatened the unity of these countries. The ancestors of the modern bourgeois—the guild masters and merchants of the cities—had supported the principle of centralization, for they needed order, stable finances, and safe roads to move their wares from one place to another.

However, when it turned out that the kings still surrounded themselves with the members of the two old estates of church and nobility and permitted the only productive estate, the middle classes, to pay, the latter rebelled. The bourgeois became the revolutionary or the "liberal" of the end of the eighteenth and the first half of the nineteenth century. But as often happens, the revolutionary did not finish his own revolution; he soon became a conservative himself. He was afraid of the rise of the Socialist tendencies of the rising working class. Especially on the Continent, but to a degree also in England, the feudal classes continued to have an influence on the political and social climate that far exceeded their numbers and the value of their contributions. They blocked the rise of talent in the higher brackets of the officialdom, the army, and even the universities. In France, a combination of military and clerical forces allowed the condemnation of the innocent Jew, Captain Dreyfus, as a spy.

In Germany and other countries a Jew could not have become an active army officer in any case, even conversion to Christianity did not open the door. Too, in the academic world and in the professions, distinctions were still made between gentiles and men of Jewish descent. And although the culture of the nation-state was definitely secular—its rise had been a continuous hot or cold war against clericalism—the churches insisted successfully on Christian instruction in the schools and were ready for battle whenever government encroached on their privileges.

After 1789, France was the main arena of religious conflict. Nevertheless, after the final separation of state and church in 1905, the French philosopher and educator Ferdinand Buisson still had to fight the belief that his country consisted of "two Frances" or "two irreconcilable races"—one secular, the other antisecular.[3]

But however serious the tensions were in the pre-World War

3. *La Foi laïque* (Paris: Hachette, 1913), p. 49. See in this context Robert Ulich, *The Education of Nations* (Cambridge: Harvard University Press), pp. 154ff.

I society of Europe, in terms of patriotism the bourgeois was second to no one. He had grown up with the state, and he lived in it, with it, and through it, like a fish in water. Because of the traditional jealousy among the nations, he could easily be persuaded to turn his aggressive instinct, which the well-established civil order no longer permitted him to direct against his neighbor, against other countries. He supported nationalist movements, praised the heroism of the army, financed enormous war budgets "for the defense of the fatherland," and looked suspiciously at any attempt to educate the young in other than strongly patriotic ideals.

Very few European nationals were good Europeans. The large majority never traveled beyond their national boundaries, physically and mentally, even if they had the means to do so. Of course, the European bourgeois was vaguely proud of having been born in an old and venerable civilization and looked down somewhat at his American counterpart (who nevertheless had so much in common with him that his descendants are today the best illustration of the bourgeois spirit). The idea of mankind as a transnational unity of human beings was foreign to him; it was little more than an abstraction or a product of dreamy idealists.

There appeared, however, one power that questioned the whole conception of capitalism, nationalism, and the state as the guarantor of human order, justice, and freedom: socialism. It first appeared in many forms—utopian, religious, or atheist— until Karl Marx brought some order into the movement by analyzing systematically the forces which, according to his opinion, form a society. He took over Hegel's idea of historical dialectics, or of the interaction of opposing forces in the development of society, but rejected his metaphysics. It is not an abstract World Mind, he said, that drives history forward, but the material conditions of living and the resulting struggle of classes. At the beginning of the new era, exploiting feudalism had been replaced by the capitalist class. Now the time had come when exploiting capitalism had to be replaced by the exploited proletariat. Then —here the empiricist historian turns into the utopian—man could live in justice and international peace.

Religion, to Marx, was the opium of the people; it diverted

them from pursuing their true interests—and so did patriotism and the adulation of the state. Rather than providing even a minimum of health, dignity, and culture to hungry and exhausted workers, governments had ordered soldiers and the police to beat down strikers and had sent their organizers to jail. From the bourgeois point of view, could one think of a more destructive demon than the Jew, Karl Marx?

So fantastic appeared his theories to the respectable professors of politics and economics that in their textbooks they ignored them or allowed them but a footnote, supposed to be sufficient to refute them forever. But neither violence nor silence, neither moral indignation nor the thunder from the pulpits, succeeded in extinguishing the sparks of subversiveness. Marxism grew, both as a theory and as a political movement, in the form of Socialist parties.

Nevertheless, until the end of World War I radical Marxism, with its postulate of the dictatorship of the proletariat, was more a verbal threat than a real danger. Despite vehement orations of agitators and outbreaks of discontent, the workers in the Western countries were not real *Klassenkaempfer* (class fighters). Public education had become more and more universal and had indoctrinated them with conformist ideas; income and the working conditions were gradually improving. And even the laboring classes, especially the women among them, were too deeply moored in the so-called Christian order to believe in the value of a totally secular formation of society. There existed many atheist and materialistic discussion clubs. Nevertheless, when their members went home, they knew what not to believe, but they did not know what to believe. Furthermore, most of them were not sufficiently schooled to discuss systematically what Feuerbach, Marx, and Darwin had really intended to say. Nor did they understand what the new "Socialist" or "proletarian culture"—a postulate of leftist intellectuals—was really going to be. They wanted reforms, not revolutions. Their dream was higher pay, better working conditions, and a better future for their children. In England and especially in the United States, revolutionary Marxism never attracted more than a small minority of the laboring classes.

The cataclysm of a world war was needed to prepare the

minds of the people for radical changes. Even then, was the social order of the bourgeois really destroyed? Riots and smaller revolutions broke out at many places, and the Continental monarchs and princes were deposed (mostly with respectful preservation of their rights of property). But the upheavals resulted more from war fatigue, defeat, and despair than from a truly revolutionary impetus with the will to bring about a new era of mankind. Some young German workers wrote beautiful revolutionary poetry, but it was read by intellectuals. There was no new "Marseillaise." Only Russia possessed the redoubtable strength to wage a civil war—out of which there developed a new political system and a new constellation of world power.

2. THE ECONOMY

Politics and economics are inseparable. Neither could exist without the other, for the state needs the taxes of the earners, and the earners need the protection of the state. However bold and foreseeing was the initiative of the bourgeois entrepreneur who risked his fortune in the opening of mines, the building of new plants, and the construction of railroads, in its initial phase every branch of modern industry owed its growth to the support of the state.

Nevertheless, the economic system of the bourgeois period worked on the assumption that it was capital, privately owned and skillfully invested, that provided the fuel for the vitality of a modern society. The fact of *private* ownership has to be emphasized, for it is not capital as such, in the sense of the aggregation of money and goods used for the production of other goods, which distinguishes a capitalist from a noncapitalist society. The distinguishing mark is the ownership of capital and the power that goes with it. As wielders of the work and wealth of the people, the Soviet and Chinese empires are the most powerful capitalists known in history, and in the Middle Ages the Catholic church possessed more property than any other organization, though the individual priest took the oath of poverty.

Nor is capitalism, in the sense of free individualistic enterprise, a new phenomenon. The ancient nations, including Greece and Rome, were capitalist, even to the degree of extending private ownership to human beings, as did the landlords of the Southern states up to the Civil War and, though in some disguise, do many owners of the large South American latifundia.

It is beyond precise verification whether, as the Marxists would assert, the economic system determines every aspect of human history, but it certainly influences man's existence more than we often assume. It is the collective expression of one of the most fundamental drives in man—the drive to survive; to earn; to consume; and, if possible, to accumulate some property.

Capital and property affect also the manner and quality of our survival: whether we will have some pictures on the wall and a vase with flowers on the table, or whether we live in an unheated cottage with a leaking roof. Although, as the homes of many parvenus prove, one cannot buy good taste with money, one can nevertheless pay an art expert and an interior decorator. And the children of the newly rich may sooner or later become the arbiters of taste and donate paintings to museums of art. Even such seemingly unmaterialistic cultural pursuits as religion, the humanistic studies, or science and education reveal the sometimes subtle and sometimes all-too-obvious influence of material force. And just as there are hierarchies in such distinct areas as ecclesiastical life, in scholarship, and in politics, there are also hierarchies in the general social order; and today more than ever, a person's social status is determined by his position on the ladder of wealth.

Only in cultures where intellectual and spiritual elements were esteemed above everything else did wealth as such play no role; in some societies, it was even regarded as degrading. The guru in the Hindu, the rabbi in the Jewish, and the monk in the Christian traditions stood outside and above the economic structure. And so, to a degree, do the artist and scholar in our time. No educated person would be particularly interested in the earnings of Albert Einstein.

But these are exceptions. The profit motive and the ensuing forms of competition have been deeply embedded in our value system. The incipient stages of the consequent style of life developed in the Renaissance, with its urban forms of investment, and in the Protestant-Calvinist era, with its emphasis on the religious value of work, thrift, and perseverance. They came to full flower in the Industrial Revolution, when only "moneyed men" could buy the instruments of production. Efficiency often became the exclusive criterion of a person, and the value of an enterprise was no longer measured in terms of its benefits for the life of an individual and his society; primarily, it was measured in economic terms—profit, production, marketing, and technical progress. The skillful entrepreneur could put to his service those large masses of people who—expropriated as a result of the decline of agriculture and the old handicrafts—had to sell simply their physical strength in order to support themselves. The new forms of production were determined by the perfection of the machine in combination with division of labor, calculated planning, and intricate organization. Furthermore, the rapidly increasing systems of transportation on land and sea, of sales organization, and of the public press required large investments, available only to the wealthy. (We have here the beginning of our present technocracy, in comparison with which, however, the business world of our grandfathers and great-grandfathers—without radio, television, the airplane, and the computer, perhaps even without telephone—makes an almost primitive impression.) The big bourgeois, that is, the factory owners, bankers, and manipulators of new markets, not only dominated the realms of commerce, but was influential as well within and behind the network of national and international politics. How little then, or even today, does the voter know what forces finally determine his and his children's future!

One cannot help asking the question: to what extent did the new economic situation, created by the bourgeois, produce a new type of man? The answer is not as simple as those who too closely relate environmental changes to personality patterns assume. There abides a center in the existence of the human species that has remained the same in its long history. Man has always been kind and cruel, greedy and generous, loving and hateful, fond of the decorative and the melodious; and he has wallowed in crime and ugliness.

Of course, with regard to the blend and mixture of our psy-

chic qualities we are different from our ancestors. The greater
latitude in style and incentives of living has made us richer in
impressions and knowledge. But has it made us more complete,
more proud, and more self-reliant? The few of us who ever sat
and talked in the old workshops of a carpenter or potter need
not be told about the difference between these now disappearing
centers of craftsmanship and a modern factory—personality in
the former, anonymity in the latter. The old craftsman determined the use of his tools and planned his work. The modern
industrial worker is determined by a machine he does not own.
His motions are not organic but restricted and automatic. He
may not even know the final purpose of his product.

In many respects, there has occurred a blunting of those
qualities which at an earlier time characterized a personality, a
sense of initiative and independence, however illusionary those
qualities may have been in many respects. Not merely the industrial worker, but to a degree even the modern teacher and
members of other mass professions, have learned that they can
succeed only through unionization. They will be inclined to
think in terms of mass interests, mass concepts, and perhaps
also mass prejudices. Their capacity for initiative will be dulled
because they cannot apply it. Endless are the numbers of frustrated men and women who have left colleges and universities
with high aspirations, only to be caught later in the inescapable
net of mass organization. Many live in dwellings which make it
difficult to create an individual home; they have to read their
house or door number in order to distinguish it from other
people's residences.

Nevertheless, much more dismal than we imagine today is,
is the picture we receive when reading the early Socialist pro-
tests against bourgeois capitalism and the humanitarian literature inspired by John Ruskin and other reformers. Almost no
exaggeration is possible when applied to the situation of workers
during the Industrial Revolution and the following decades.
Between the end of the Napoleonic Wars and the rise of labor
self-help and labor legislation, the workman was more cruelly
exploited than slaves in antiquity had been.

Nowhere was the onslaught of uncontrolled laissez faire en-

terprise on the working classes as catastrophic as in the rapidly
industrialized cities of England. In order to subsist, whole
families, including children, had to work in narrow rows of
workbenches at spinning jennies from twelve to eighteen hours
a day. They were punished with exacting fines if they were only
a few minutes late. Some mill owners boasted that they made
large sums annually by "two descriptions of clocks"; and children and women were severely beaten before their companions.
Of 1,079 persons employed in a flax mill of Leeds only 9 at-
tained the age of fifty and only 22 the age of forty. These data
are taken from a speech of Michael Thomas Sadler delivered in
1831 in Parliament to disprove the employers' arguments against
government interference.[4] As late as 1867 the English trade
unions were illegal. Not before the early 1870s did the English
courts change the laws and allow peaceful picketing.

The history of France, the land of the classic bourgeois with
his well-known motto "get rich quick," has been full of cruel
persecutions of workers. And in American history books we read
of the Haymarket Riot in the Chicago of 1886 and of the ensuing trial at which a packed jury held eight anarchists responsible for the fatal throwing of a bomb—though those that were
not executed were later pardoned.

In Germany, Bismarck tried to stem the growth of the
workers' movement partly by the enactment of social legislature
in the form of health, accident, disablement, and old-age insur-
ance. But his motives were not merely charitable. He tried,
though in vain, to weed out the germs of socialism by means of
a law against the Social Democratic party, which was supported
not only by the conservative but also by the liberal parties. At
the same time, the emperor William II took it for granted that
his troops could be used to shoot striking workers, until, at the
beginning of World War I, he deigned to include the Social
Democrats, whom he had previously called "*vaterlandslose
Gesellen*" (vagabonds without a country), among the decent
citizens. His majesty needed the strength of their labor for the
fields of battle and for the armament industry.

4. See Robert Ulich, *The Education of Nations* (Cambridge: Harvard
University Press, 1961), p. 103.

As in modern depressions, during the bourgeois period the working classes were especially hard hit by economic crises, whereas a prudent wealthy man, even if his business suffered, could rely to an extent on his capital resources. Some even profited from bankruptcy. As in politics, in the economic sphere the boundaries between the upper middle class and the old aristocracy of birth began to blur, especially in England where only the oldest son of the family inherited the title. However, when possible, a member of the old Continental nobility liked to see his children married within the caste, though the richer burse of the new bourgeois relative might have given him some comfort. A surprising number of Prussian noblemen married into Jewish families. The more affluent and enterprising of the aristocracy themselves went into business, becoming large-scale producers or investors in commercial ventures such as speculation in real estate, food, wineries, and breweries.

Furthermore, after the bourgeois had arrived at his place in the social structure, he had many things in common with the old conservatives, especially the fear that the growth of labor, or the "fourth estate," might disturb the newly established social equilibrium. More and more he veered from the anticonservative and liberal ideology of the Enlightenment toward conventional modes of living and thinking. It disturbed him to be reminded by the leaders of labor that in the revolutions against feudalism of 1789, 1830, and 1848, rugged men with sooty hands and linen blouses had done most of the fighting on the barricades of "liberty, fraternity, and equality," only to be cheated when some success had been achieved by the "third estate" and the streets were quiet again.

The picture which the industrial proletariat offered to the society of the nineteenth century explains the horror with which insecure lower-middle-class people spoke of the danger of "sinking down into the proletariat" and their desperately conservative reaction against new methods of production and salesmanship which ruined their antiquated business. Hitler found his first large following among small-scale store owners and dispossessed craftsmen. They were also open to the worst kind of anti-Semitism, for the new, big, efficient department stores were mostly

Jewish owned. And do we need a more vivid reminder of the impact of the deracination of the poor from the natural soil of living than our modern city slums?

The close connection of the value system of the bourgeois with his purse and ledger should save us from illusions about one of his central ideological concepts—the concept of freedom.[5] (When I applied at an American consulate in Canada for American citizenship, the first question asked by the young consul was "What are you worth?" I still was old-fashioned enough to need an explanation of the meaning of my "worth." My first answer had been that I had to leave the judgment on this point to my friends.) In England, political freedom had been for a long time understood as the right of Parliament to prevent the crown from impinging on the money of the taxpayer, and it is no mere accident that the American Revolution started with differences of opinion concerning the rights of the English to lay taxes on such precious commodities as tea and rum. Certainly, that is not the whole story; only in long and heroic battles did the founders of modern republicanism win the rights of freedom of expression and thought, of vote and assembly, of just process of law, and of political representation. Nevertheless, prominent members of the bourgeoisie, not to speak of the old nobility, were by no means inclined to extend these privileges beyond the boundaries of class and nation. The poorer classes were for a long time excluded from the full rights of citizenship, especially from the right to vote. When the workmen knocked at the door, it was called insurrection. In the United States, we are only beginning to allow the black the right of full citizenship guaranteed by the Constitution.

This monopolistic claim of the wealthy, together with the

5. How deeply we are still in that state of mind may be concluded from Leo Perla's book *Can We End the Cold War? A Study of American Foreign Policy* (New York: Macmillan, 1960). There he describes (perhaps somewhat distortingly, but not entirely incorrectly) the hierarchy of the American value system in the following order: (1) money, (2) power, (3) material possessions, (4) cleanliness, (5) intelligence and education, and (6) moral qualities. See George S. Counts, "Where Are We?," *The Education Forum* (May, 1966).

prevalence of the acquisitive motive, leads us to another shadowy side of early bourgeois liberalism—colonialism, or the exploitation of the economically retarded countries.

Colonialism, or, as it has also been called, "economic imperialism," was strongly defended by the economists of the time. In his "Principles of Political Economy" (1848), J. S. Mill declared: "Colonialism in the present state of the world, is the best affair of business in which an old and wealthy country can engage." [6]

Although economists have expressed different opinions about the causes and motives of this phase of modern history, they all, whether Marxist, neo-Marxist, or conservative, have been influenced by Lenin's famous essay on "Imperialism, the Highest Stage of Capitalism," published in 1917. World War I heralded for him the victory of communism over the acquisitive and nationalist bourgeois system.

Like capitalism, colonialism is by no means a modern invention. It was practiced by ancient Tyre, Carthage, and the Greek city-states. A new phase of colonialism originated with the discovery of new continents during the fifteenth and sixteenth centuries. But whereas Spain and Portugal, to the detriment of their own productivity, were primarily interested in importing gold and other goods, modern colonialism as practiced by other Western nations became a means to lighten the overproduction of material at home, to relieve overpopulation, and to secure bases for international commerce. The colonists were expected and even forced to trade primarily with the homeland. Indeed, the English colonists made their mother tongue the international means of communication.

There were also strategic considerations. For example, England occupied the coastal regions of West Africa in order to secure the dominance of its navy in the Atlantic. Furthermore, just as the Spanish Catholic clergy of the sixteenth century followed the warriors of Cortes in order to wrest the souls of the heathens from the grip of the devil, so also the other churches

6. London: Longmans, Green, 1909, p. 727. See also Bernard Semme, "On the Economics of 'Imperialism,'" in *Economics and the Idea of Mankind*, ed. Bert Hoselitz (New York: Columbia University Press, 1965).

did not wish to leave the "pagans" in eternal terror—although many of them had a religious heritage older, and certainly in depth not inferior, to theirs.

Today, colonial imperialism seems to belong to the past. It vanished with the self-destruction of Old Europe during the world wars and with the concomitant rise of new national states on the continents of Asia and Africa. (Paradoxically, these states owe much to Hitler!) However, the odious tangle of paternalism, militarism, and superiority complexes survives in the struggle of the bigger powers for the dominance of smaller and often helpless territories. The United States claims to protect the emerging states against Communist invasion, whereas the Communists claim to liberate them from the evils of capitalism.

Just as tragic is the fact that the memory of colonial times still remains a sting to the pride of the inhabitants of former colonies and a blemish on the reputation of the so-called Christian nations. In the Western nations, and even there only to a degree, it required decades—under the influence of American economic literature—for the term "capitalism" to lose its negative connotation. In the Soviet domain and in many countries of East Asia and of Africa it still carries the meaning of exploitation of the weak by the strong.

Yet, the modern tendency to see nothing but evil in the industrial system of the bourgeois is lopsided. At home, the health of the population (which also in the rural districts had been deplorable) gradually improved as a result of medical research and humanitarian movements. In spite of initial attempts at suppression, one of the greatest achievements of the modern age, the self-help of the underpaid through collective action, became in the course of time an acknowledged fact.

Furthermore, more than anything else, the new economic system broke the static character of European society. Individual initiative and intelligence were increasingly appreciated; a craftsman of exceptional skill and initiative could become a manufacturer, and his children could go to the universities. Some could even become officers in the army and officials in the ministries. Much could be achieved with money. But unfortunately, instead of being valued as a means, it often became an end in itself.

As with the abuses of labor, the bourgeois period provided its own correctives to the injustices of colonialism. When the most cruel forms of the exploitation of natives became widely known (especially the Belgian reign of terror in the Congo), humanitarian movements arose, and thousands of native Africans and Asians were educated at Western universities. It became increasingly difficult for the white man to defend colonial abuses with the assertion that he gave an "inferior breed of humanity" work and a sense of order. (Many industrialists excused the labor conditions in their own country with similar reasons.) And without in the least excusing the sins of the "master races," one must also concede that the opening of unknown continents was an inevitable phase in man's widening conquest of the world. The human being is an aggressive animal with a dislike for empty spaces.

Nor should we forget that the brutality of the strong and the suffering of the weak in Africa and Asia was—on the whole —even greater during the precolonial than during the colonial period. The white powers and their missionaries forced certain countries to abolish at least the most inhuman customs and superstitions. One has but to read the books by Henry Morton Stanley to imagine the barbaric conditions imposed on the native populations by their own masters.[7] At the end of the nineteenth century, an Indian widow was no longer burned on her husband's funeral pyre; cannibalism had almost disappeared; and, owing to the English fleet, African chieftains could no longer sell their captives or tribesmen to slave traders.

The colonizing nations, especially Britain, developed the resources of the overseas territories; without their organizing zeal, the formerly subjected countries would be even less competent to rule themselves than several of them are today. In some new nations many of the older inhabitants, among them even those who fought the battle of independence, now ask themselves

7. *Slavery and Slave Trade in Africa* (New York, 1893).

whether they felt more secure under foreign rule or under the continual turmoil of revolutions at home.

Nevertheless, there would have been fewer of these revolutions if the colonial powers had not so arbitrarily divided the subjected continents into unnatural political entities. The worst one can say about the political-economic system of the bourgeois is this: he failed to transfer the spirit of enlightenment and rationality, bequeathed to him by the eighteenth century, into national and international life. Rather, he intensified the collective-aggressive instincts in man, the fury of which was shown in full force in the two world wars.

The untamed master spirit of Western man is evident even to the superficial observer. Besides the theaters, concert halls, libraries, museums, and picture galleries which adorn the old centers of the European capitals, we find an endless number of monuments dedicated to the most ruthless suppressors of the freedom and happiness of peoples of other nations. It is a weak excuse for this exhibition of aggressiveness that war and conquest have also been the media of mass migrations and of economic and cultural contacts of the peoples of the world. One might have had it by more civilized means; the price was too high.

Chapter 2

RELIGION, HUMANISM, AND EDUCATION

1. RELIGION

Although the conversations of the middle classes turned mainly around politics and business, religion was also a favorite theme. It provided a feeling of spiritual security, of some meaning that transcended the hustle and bustle in office and factory, of human brotherhood—at least on Sunday morning—and of belonging to a well-ordered universe. Furthermore, religion and piety were thought to be the best defense against the increasing threats of relativism and immorality among the masses and even among the educated. Finally, religion provided a father image that lifted man gently above the threatening fog of loneliness within a competitive and noisy world. It also gave the pious a certain hope for salvation after the journey through this valley of finitude. Perhaps, in the world beyond he might also meet the beloved he had lost, and as a man of righteousness, he was certain that the meeting would take place in heavenly surroundings. Pictures of hellfire gradually disappeared from the sermons of urbane priests and ministers. In religion one also appreciated the elements of cult, art, and inspiration—things for which otherwise there was precious little time.

No doubt, Christianity, as well as Judaism among many Western Jews, was more a conventional way of life than a burning conviction. Faith no longer flowed from the depths of the soul; it failed to cause either the exaltation of heavenly vision or the anguish of sleepless nights about which we read in the diaries of older times. Prayer was considered a good habit, though it could not be proved that it increased productivity.

Protestants read the Bible with its praise of the poor and the condemnation of the moneymakers; Catholics, too, heard the parable of the rich, the camel, and the eye of the needle. But both steadfastly refused to recognize that Jesus was a revolutionary. And the socially well-integrated clergy did little or nothing to correct the false image of the carpenter's son whose followers undermined the Roman Empire. To quarrel about denominational differences was a sign of bad breeding. Only when such differences had political background, such as Bismarck's *Kulturkampf*, hostilities arose. One supported richly the Christian missions in foreign lands, though often for causes that were tinged with moral and racial arrogance.

However, though the official trademark of the Western nations was "Christian," secularization had progressed far. In fact, the nineteenth century was a lull in the life of Christianity. The more sophisticated already suspected voluntary martyrdom as a sign of a psychopathic trend. Directly or indirectly, they were influenced by David Friedrich Strauss's *Das Leben Jesu* and Ernest Renan's *La Vie de Jésus;* both described the prophet as a human being, divinely inspired, but nevertheless natural.

One could even venture the statement that the well-educated bourgeois was more interested in religion when it was criticized than when it was defended. Many people like to watch the demolition of an old building, for the destructive fascinates them. On a higher intellectual level, one quoted Montaigne's *Aphorisms* and Voltaire's *Candide*. Herbert Spencer expressed the opinion of many university graduates when, in his *Synthetic Philosophy* of 1885, he concluded that all religions intuited that there was some ultimate element of force, energy, or power behind the mental and physical phenomena of life. But these intuitions, so he said, were still clouded in anthropomorphic superstitions, incompatible with the modern scientific mind. Man should live in a form of religious reverence growing out of the certainty of the presence of an "Infinite Eternal Energy" from which all things derive. More, according to Spencer, cannot be said. The "Great Enigma" would never be solved.

While Herbert Spencer and a thinker of similar bent, the Frenchman Auguste Comte, argued on a level too high for the ordinary reader, the German biologist Ernst Haeckel, ardent apostle of Darwinism, used in his *Welträtsel* of 1899 (published the following year in England under the title *The Riddle of the Universe*) a vocabulary crude enough to recommend his materialistic monism as the new synthesis of science and enlightened religion. Monist circles were founded in many countries, often frequented by intellectually somewhat advanced Socialist workers. Though unprepared for critical philosophical discussion, they felt elated by the hitherto nonexistent chance to participate in the free exchange of ideas. The more they discussed, the more they believed that the churches, while preaching mercy and brotherhood, had been the allies of capitalism, militarism, superstition, and social injustice.

But it is perhaps still more difficult to generalize about the religious attitude of the working population of the prewar period than about the attitude of the middle classes. In the Anglo-Saxon countries, atheist Marxism existed only sporadically. Only in France, Germany, and Austria, and, needless to say, among the Russian revolutionaries did it become a kind of Weltanschaung. Even there the Catholic labor unions kept their members close to the Roman hierarchy which, warned by the rapid growth of skepticism and the Socialist parties, became critical of the growing influence of the worldly powers of money and nationalist politics. An outcry of indignation arose within the enterpreneurial class when, in 1891, Pope Leo XIII issued the encyclical *Rerum Novarum*, which recommended a Christian form of economic solidarism instead of the dominating systems of capitalist competition on the one side and Socialist atheism on the other. Unfortunately, the Protestant churches kept silent. They did not dare offend the ruling powers.

Much of this belongs to the past. But still unforgotten and even growing in significance because it reaches much deeper into the human soul than outward influences can ever do is the work of three thinkers whose existence can be described as a searching dialogue between man and his self: the Dane Soren Kierkegaard; the German, Friedrich Nietzsche; and the Austrian, Sigmund Freud. No doubt, younger men of the educated group were profoundly impressed by the thought of the three men.

Nevertheless, the optimism of the bourgeois prevailed equally against the Christian anguish of Kierkegaard, the superhuman romanticism of Nietzsche, and the depth psychology of Freud. Nor made the skepticism of the empiricist and Marxist philosophers a deep impression. Like all healthy people, the bourgeois had a great talent for balancing or ignoring extremes when they threatened his equilibrium. After all, what alternatives did the critics have to offer? They all seemed uninviting to the respectable citizen. He felt instinctively that modernity, perhaps just because of its scientific progress, offered no valid substitutes for the old symbols of reverence. Thus, he preferred Christianity. And where the urge had lost breath, artificial respiration was easily available. One idolized the national flag and gathered for marching, wining, dining, and fulminating oratory at patriotic festivals—not forgetting occasional invocations of the Almighty who was credited with always being on the side of the just—and the just, of course, was always one's own nation. Only Socialists, anarchists, and freethinkers—all men without God and Church—dared sneer at such expressions of national elation. Good men avoided their company. State and church symbolized order, protected property, and was the source of morality and good manners. Why fight such a useful institution? In Gustave Flaubert's novel *L'Education sentimentale*, a worthless bon vivant rebukes a cynical remark about Christianity with the assertion *"qu'on devait respecter la religion."*

Despite a galaxy of great scholars who had pointed at the depth of Buddhism and Confucianism, and desipte Schopenhauer's rather serious romance with the Nirvana idea, one was convinced that in his infinite wisdom the Lord had created Christianity in order to document the superiority of Western culture. Even today, many a good Christian is a bit offended when told that, religiously speaking, he lives on borrowed capital, imported from Asia. He forgets that the development of the old mythical lore of his faraway pagan ancestors—full of barbaric fierceness but also of profound wisdom—was once arrested by Christian missionaries and their political supporters. Sometimes, the adoption of the new gospel was gratefully received; often, it was accomplished by force.

Has the conversion really succeeded? This problem bothered the christianized Jew, Heinrich Heine, who, a hundred years before Hitler, in 1835, concluded his essay on the history of religion and philosophy in Germany with the following words:

> Christianity—and this is its finest merit—has somewhat succeeded in appeasing the savage Germanic lust of fighting. However, it was not strong enough to exterminate it for ever. And if sometime the taming talisman, the cross, will break, then again we will hear the clashing ferocity of battle, that insane berserk rage of which the old Nordic poets sing and chant.
>
> The talisman is now rotting, and the day will come when it crumbles. Then the old idols will rise from the dust of the past and rub the thorns and years old earth from their eyes, and Thor with his giant hammer will leap up and smite the gothic cathedrals.[1]

Unfortunately, the saddening discrepancy between religious confession and moral commitment applies to all peoples and cultures, whether Hindu, Buddhist, Islamic, or Christian. In the Victorian era, English "Christian gentlemen," partly in their French counterparts, waged shameful wars against the helpless Chinese in order to prevent them from stopping the cultivation and trade of opium and thus to forestall the poisoning of millions. When, after World War II, the India of Gandhi was liberated from foreign rule, the principle of tolerance and non-violence was forgotten. Buddhists and Moslems slaughtered each other with guns, stones, and daggers. The sadist in the human being may even hide behind the Bible and thus, with a good conscience, apply the torture and the stake against the heretic or forcefully expel whole populations from their native land. To the historian, mankind may sometimes appear like a

1. "Zur Geschichte der Religion and Philosophie in Deutschland" in *Heinrich Heine, Zur Geschichte der Deutschen Philosophie*, ed. Wolfgang Harich (Berlin: Aufbau, 1956), p. 183.

herd of cattle which a sudden danger, even imagined, or a wild bull, may turn into a tornado. Freud's dark id is still more powerful than the superego. It is also difficult to dismiss Carl Jung's idea of the collective unconsciousness as mere speculation. The barbarism of our remote ancestors seems still to brood in the dark corners of the human soul. To make the human being humane, more is necessary than religion. Will we ever succeed?

2. HUMANISM

Besides his religious tradition, the bourgeois had a long humanist heritage. Sometimes the two trends of thought were inimical, sometimes tolerant, and sometimes invading, for the borders between religion and humanism are difficult to define. As we speak of humanist forms of religion, so we speak also of religious forms of humanism. Nevertheless, there are decisive differences.

A truly pious Christian knows himself to be in the hands of God. From the joyful security of divine protection he may plunge into the despair of utter failure in the eyes of the Ultimate. Even man's virtues, so Luther believed with Saint Paul, count for nothing before the stern glory of the omniscient Judge who searches deeper into our hearts than we ourselves can do. God turns the wheel of destiny. "What is man," says the psalmist, "that thou are mindful of him?"

For the humanist, the center of gravity shifts from world transcendence to world immanence. But even in this respect, doubts may be raised. The greatest humanists, such as Michel Montaigne, Wolfgang Goethe, Herbert Spencer, or William James, are strangely self-contradictory. For them, life is too rich to be pressed into logical categories. Standing in awe before the universal wholeness that expresses itself through an infinitude of shapes and shades, they leave it to minor minds to submit to the tyranny of definitions, which—necessary though they are in our analytical attempts—obscure the full view of reality. No doubt, the lack of a canon will keep the humanist, as every truly liberal man, at a certain disadvantage in comparison with the believers in dogma, who have always been in the majority because of man's preference for the comfort of certitude, however unexamined, over the strain of search and self-examination.

One consideration alone should caution us against conventional labels. Religious writers often object to the ego centeredness of the humanist attitude. However, Christianity, preoccupied as it is with man's nature, salvation, and personal immortality, could be interpreted as the most extreme form of human self-interest. André Gide rightly called Christianity an incomparable school of individualization, with every one more precious than the other. Opinions may differ as to whether or not this is praise. But certainly, in comparison with the self-concern of *homo religiosus*, the humanist, with his inclination toward agnosticism, is a modest and self-renunciating man. Although he puts much value on the perfection of his personality, he does not expect the whole universe to resolve around his unique self, here and hereafter. The aim of the Christian, as it was often expressed in earlier times—to become godlike—seems to the humanist the height of arrogance.

Whereas all the great world religions come from the brooding transcendentalism of the Asiatic soul, humanism was born in the clear air of Greece. Belief in the human figure, the human face, the human beings, and the gods (with the god sometimes being more human than the human beings), the human community, the genius of man branching into art, philosophy and nature—all that happened separately also in other ancient cultures. But in its combination and culmination, it is Greek. Hence, whenever Western men were humanists, anxious to search into themselves and the world, and unhampered by the prejudices of the time, and whenever they spoke of the dignity, but also of the perils of human existence, they reverted to the Greeks: to Plato and Aristotle, Pythagoras and Archimedes, to Aeschylus and Sophocles.

Even Christian theology absorbed some of the ancient Greek-Roman humanism. The Neoplatonic concept of the divine *Logos* as the principle or cosmic order appears in the first sentences of the Epistle according to Saint John. The Stoic postulate of the superiority of reason over the struggle of the emotions, as well as certain parts of the Greek-Roman philosophy of nature and society, impressed the more tolerant of the Church Fathers. At the height of the Middle Ages, during the flowering of Scholasticism, Aristotle became "the teacher" of Albert of Cologne, Thomas Aquinas, and their successors. But inevitably, the gap remained between the Christian concept of the *ratio divina*, expressing itself through the miracle of revelation, and of the *ratio humana*, seeking truth without supernatural premises. The premise of the two still constitutes the difference between the Christian and the humanist attitude.

World-immanent humanism appeared for the first after Christ in the Renaissance. The leaders of the Renaissance were Platonic and mystically minded pantheists; they delved with unlimited curiosity into the obscurities of the Cabala, or they conducted physical experiments in their academies and in the friendly intellectual climate of the north Italian universities, with Copernicus and Galileo among them. They were captivated by everything that promised to lead them deeper into the beauty and depth of human and natural life. Like adolescents, they were sensuous and pondering, aggressive and uncertain at the same time. Although some of them were heretics in the eyes of the church—which was then more tolerant about human errors and vices than it was in later centuries—most of them remained within the embrace of Christianity. Nevertheless, they initiated the gradual transition from medieval transcendentalism to modern secularity. They changed man's ideas about the aims of life and about the position of his planet and of himself in the cosmic order. They also insisted on the right and freedom of independent research, or, as Spinoza called it later, the idea of *libertas philosophandi*.

At the same time, the sons of the privileged families decided to leave the Christian virtue of humility (never a peculiarity of the influential) to priests and servants and searched for a life of glory. An elite of intelligence established itself alongside the old estates of the clergy and the nobility; and if the ultimate goal of Christian man was immortality (who could prove it anyhow?), there was immortality also in a life creatively planned, boldly pursued, rich in adventure, appreciative of the beauty of art and of ideas, something finished and completed in itself: the educated gentleman replaced the saint.

But after a century of humanistic exuberance, control over the soul of man again fell into the hands of the clergy. Under the pressure of the Reformation and the Counter Reformation the students in the Protestant academies and the Catholic colleges delivered flamboyant orations in Latin and Greek (on the Protestant side even in Hebrew), about the ancient virtues of wisdom, temperance, justice, and fortitude as steps toward the Christian virtues of faith, hope, and charity. At the same time, they pitilessly condemned the heresies of any other faith.

Yet even the clergy felt obliged to adopt certain features of the Renaissance. The young nobles were allowed a large amount of freedom for chivalrous exercises. Christian *pietas* was blended with the art of *eloquentia*, which, in the tradition of the Roman Quintilian, became the symbolic term of both elegance in speech and excellence in conduct. This, after all, was neither Christianity pure and simple nor the secular humanism of the ancients and of the Renaissance; it was a mixture of both: Christian humanism. Certainly a compromise, conflicting and ambiguous in many respects and not free from aspects of showmanship.

However, some people, especially poets, could not be so easily tamed. They still indulged in a romantic longing for genuine heathendon. They wanted to be away from all the trivialities of society, from the orthodoxies and heterodoxies of Christianity, from all the bigotry and the black robes of the clergy, and out into the blue skies, the mountains, and the temples of Greece and Italy! Indeed, we owe some of the finest poetry to this neoclassical humanism, which lasted to the middle of the nineteenth century—the most productive form of escapism from the grip of dull reality the world has seen. It flowered especially in Germany, where religious intolerance and hundreds of petty principalities fettered the minds of the creative. There Goethe, Schiller, and Hölderlin were longing for a new harmony between soul and body, nature and reason, eros and purity, individualism and society. In England we find the same nostalgic feeling in the works of Lord George Byron, Samuel Coleridge,

Percy Bysshe Shelley, Matthew Arnold, and William Wordsworth. These poets expressed little sympathy for the kind of
shallow eighteenth-century rationalism that explained the romantic mystery of life by platitudinous common sense. Nevertheless, the greatest among them could not have expressed their
inner life without the preceding liberalization of the mind
initiated by the great leaders of the rationalist movement—the
Enlightenment. For to no other group of thinkers does modern
humanism, whether poetic, intuitive, and introvert or scholarly,
scientific, and social, owe so much as to Locke and Hume, to the
bold authors of the *Encyclopédie française,* to Voltaire, Rousseau
(this inextricable bundle of fiery emotionalism and cool reason-
ing), and finally to Kant, the critic of all critiques, even his own.

The leaders of the French Revolution were also humanists,
spicing their harangues with quotations from the ancients, whom
they revered as the fathers of republicanism. Thus, since about
1800, humanism had become so rich that it more and more defies
attempts at rigid classification. It was science and radical inquiry
on the one hand, inwardness and poetic intuition on the other.

No doubt, whatever the defects of the era of the bourgeois,
it harbored a considerable number of men of high cultural
standard. They could be intensely interested in politics but also
read poetry. They could be shrewd bankers and industrial organizers but live an almost ascetic life in very modest offices. They
could choose the pessimist Schopenhauer as their philosopher
but also believe in progress. There were, of course, still bumps
and ruts ahead, but the road was clear: man, the master of the
earth (the white man in the vanguard) would also become the
master of himself. And a purified, liberal, and not-too-severe
Christianity would support his endeavors. Furthermore, much
though one was shocked by the Darwinian theory of man's
descendance, one could also turn it into an attitude of optimism
—man as the culmination of millennia of nature's struggle for
integration and self-consciousnes.

Was this bourgeois capacity of overlooking seemingly un-
bridgeable contrasts a sign of shallowness? It was and it was not.
Every civilization (as every healthy person) that wants to survive within a welter of conflicting challenges creates a concep-

tion of purpose, supported by an ideology. To the theoretician, such an ideology appears logically, even ethically, of dubious value. But it works. It is the pragmatic requirement of survival. Why should the dynamic society of the bourgeois not have hoped that the progress of man, which the Christian saw in his pilgrimage toward a supernatural heaven, be turned into a pilgrimage toward higher standards of earthly living—or toward a full and secular humanism? Even our present churches have adopted a good deal of that faith in order to hold their place in the community of modern man.

And let us not forget that besides the happy compromisers there were humanists who, because of their very concern with man's secular existence and not with a world beyond, were driven by a deep moral desire to apply the religious idea of the brotherhood and dignity of man to practical situations. They demanded the improvement of the life of the poor at home and in the colonies. They insisted on the reform of penal laws, of prisons, of hospitals for the insane, of political institutions and constitutions, and last, but not least, on the emancipation of women, even against women.

The standards which today we like to connect with the term democracy were partly created and put into effect by these men of humanist conviction; in the United States, by such personalities as Benjamin Franklin, Thomas Jefferson, John Quincy Adams, Franklin D. Roosevelt, and by those statesmen who insisted on modern legislation to protect the indigent and the old and the racial minorities.

Certainly, men of social conscience existed long before the bourgeois appeared. But while it was then mostly "charity" with all its unpleasant connotations, it has now become a moral obligation.

Needless to say, all these men looked also toward education as a means of progress.

3. EDUCATION

The institution that provided a degree of unity between the various components of the pre-World War I society was education. One may argue whether it furnished a medium for free personal culture, but it certainly was a medium of indoctrination and conformity. Elementary schools, together with some additional vocational classes, were the only educational institutions for the overwhelming majority of the people, perhaps 90 percent. They provided a modicum of knowledge by teaching the three Rs; they gave their pupils an idea of national literature, folklore, and history as well as of mathematics and the natural sciences; they imbued the people with a sense of work, thrift, and order; and they taught them the virtues (and the vices) of patriotism. Of course, there was also a good deal of religious instruction. Patriotism and religion were regarded as the indispensable foundation of all learning and morality. Even in nations without public religious instruction, as in France after 1905 and in the United States, the schools were "Christian."

In its insistence on universal literacy, Germany was ahead of the other countries; England was behind. Not before the passing of the two education laws of 1870 and 1876, which coincided with the legal recognition of the labor unions, did the English government accept the guardianship of its children's education.

Several factors converged to bring about the institution of a universal and free popular education. On the one side, the so-called lower ranks demanded more and better schooling. They no longer wished to be considered the sediment of civilization, the gray and inarticulate mass at the bottom, or "the rest," as John Locke (otherwise one of the champions of modern republicanism) had said in the second half of the sevententh century. They had learned how to organize political parties and labor unions and had begun to send representatives to Parliament.

Behind the dais in the conference halls of the workmen of Continental Europe there hung a huge red banner with the emblem "Knowledge Is Power." Some knowledge, so even the conservative governments thought, was desirable. But for what did the workers intend to use it? It became of crucial importance that the new thirst for knowledge be directed into proper channels, away from the demons of revolution and atheism toward the "perennial values of humanity." During and after the Holy Alliance between the monarchs of Austria, Prussia, and Russia, who had defeated the upstart Napoleon, even the seminars of the folkschool teachers and the new kindergartens became suspect. One did not like the idea that they were under the spiritual influence of such men as the rebellious Swiss republican Pestalozzi and the German pantheist Froebel, whose nephew had been in prison because of his liberal convictions.

But there soon appeared much more dangerous individuals, such as Marx as well as Kropotkin, Bakunin, and other exiled Russians (all conveniently lumped together as Socialists and anarchists). Their books were too difficult to be widely read. Yet, in some underground fashion (as "subversive" ideas always do), their viewpoints crept into the conversations of the people and became dangerous. Some desperadoes had even learned how to use bombs and bullets, and if they had nothing else, they used knives. The Russian Czar Alexander II was killed in 1881, and between 1894 and 1901 anarchists murdered Sadi Carnot, president of France; the much-admired empress of Austria, Elizabeth; Humbert I, king of Italy; and William McKinley, president of the United States. It had become dangerous to ride around in state equipages.

Thus even those reactionaries who had previously insisted that the poor be kept in their divinely ordered place and that the best way to govern them was to keep them ignorant began to support their governments' endeavor to make the schools a bulwark against subversiveness. Furthermore, industry and commerce needed men with some training, and so did the military which complained that some recruits from remote rural areas could neither read orders nor even distinguish between right and left.

But not merely egotistic motives aided the cause of education. The humanitarian appreciation of the value of the human person, irrespective of birth and rank, began to penetrate the conscience of the upper classes. In contrast to Voltaire, who thought of a world conveniently divided into the educated who ruled and the uneducated who had to obey and to believe in God, one now had a wider concept of a decent society. God, or Nature, had endowed all men—or at least most men—with reason; to neglect it was not merely dangerous but immoral.

Though bourgeois society raised the general level of education to heights previously unknown—universal education became the mark of a civilized nation—the bourgeois class was by no means inclined toward leveling. Those who dared talk of the right of equal education for everybody were readily accused of Socialist egalitarianism (socialistische Gleichmacherei). The class structure of the society was clearly reflected in the structure of the educational system, divided into the already described folk school for the common man and a highly selective secondary system for the privileged. Within this system, the gymnasia in Germany and in most eastern countries, the lycées in France, and the fashionable public schools in England prepared for the professions. Even for those pupils who did not enter the universities, these schools procured the general education and the prestige necessary for life in the upper social strata. They also gave their graduates the much-coveted privilege of serving as officers or reserve officers in the army.

The intellectual requirements in these upper schools were high; many students had to repeat one or two forms; the number of dropouts and repeaters amounted to 40 to 50 percent. About 1900 only about 3 to 5 percent of the Continental school population attended these schools; in England, it was even less.[2] But the small number of graduates from the selective high schools and the still smaller number of university graduates sufficed to feed the professions. The staggering increase of higher-level careers in public administration, business, and especially in the theoretical and applied sciences had not yet taken place.

It illustrates the conservative attitude of the bourgeois that, at least up to 1900, he defended the old classical subjects of Greek and Latin as the best preparation for his children. The teaching body of the older classical schools mirrored the hierarchy of learning. The teachers of the ancient languages were on the top, and the principal rose from their ranks—in England, he often came from the clergy. Then came the teachers of modern languages, of mathematics and the sciences, and finally, benev-

2. For a more detailed description of the school situation in Europe, see Robert Ulich, *The Education of Nations* (Cambridge: Harvard University Press, 1961).

olently treated but never invited to parties and conferences, the teachers of gymnastics and of the visual arts (if any were taught). Mysteriously, often the two assignments were combined. Anyone who could teach youngsters how to jump over a vaulting horse could also teach them how to copy an old Greek sculpture—presented either two-dimensionally or in the form of a dirty plaster imitation. Only in the schools for the English aristocracy, such as Eton, Harrow, and Winchester, was sport respected as a means of moral education. From them came the term "sportsmanship."

However, the intellectual and technological developments of the late nineteenth century had already engendered some severe criticism of the old classical schools. Indeed, such schools were a retarding element; they had not changed much in either content or structure since the Reformation and the Counter Reformation. But they were defended with religious zeal by the representatives of the old humanities; by the conservative parties, including the churches; and by the majority of the university professors who liked to teach a homogeneously educated corps of students. Even mathematicians and scientists preferred young scholars with a broad historical and linguistic foundation to premature specialists. The latter had often to unlearn during the first year of their higher studies what they had been taught by ambitious secondary-school teachers who, after decades spent in the classroom, had lost contact with the expanding frontiers of research. After all, the great mathematicians of the eighteenth and nineteenth centuries had gone through humanistic schools, a fact that may explain why many of them were at the same time creative writers in the fields other than their specialty, particularly in philosophy.

Let us, therefore, be just and not identify all opposition against the modernization of the secondary schools with social reaction. Was there ever an educational controversy without an admixture of egotistic interests, whether they came from the Right or from the Left? Even if imperfectly and pedantically taught—pedantry and faith in the power of words is the eternal curse of the teacher—the old humanities widened the student's horizon beyond his immediate environment. They were, so to speak, the forerunners of our modern comparative studies: to begin there meant to begin with the roots, thought to be the best means of understanding later developments. Therefore, many of the older, now disappearing, Europeans who curse the rigid teaching of the old classical school are nevertheless grateful for having gone through the torture.

Ancient literature contained models of noble conduct and heroism as well as models of style and expression. Certainly, snobbishness played a role when our grandfathers quoted the ancient authors, but there was more to it. They found in the great classical poets and thinkers a clear conception of human existence—proudly world immanent in contrast to transcendental and dualistic Christianity: the image of a person who, unafraid of the risks of a public and responsible life, tries to mold his intellect and his emotions into a self-directing and harmonious whole. This was, in essence, the Stoic-Ciceronian concept of *humanitas,* born at the time when the educated Greeks and Romans conceived of a supernational and superracial community of men, a vision destroyed by political disintegration and finally by the onslaught of barbaric masses. Every great moral vision refuses to be tied to a particular group and locality; every relapse in civilization is a loss of wholeness. To this extent, the classics—when taught by inspiring teachers, who, unfortunately, were rare—constituted a continual attempt to renew the dream of universality.

Translated into modern terms, *humanitas* is the equivalent of the "gentleman ideal," freed from its original ethnic origin within the English nation, and especially from the vice of snobbishness. But although true gentlemen like tradition and a degree of conformity, their gentleness need not prevent them from being critical and even unbending when higher issues are at stake.

And here lies the failure of the educational system of the bourgeois. Though he was originaly a rebel against feudal and ecclesiastical prejudices, when the bourgeois arrived, he became conservative. Certainly, the upper grades of the secondary schools and especially the universities discussed the secularism of the Renaissance, the defiant attitude of Martin Luther, and the ideas and social upheavals that brought about the French Revolution and the idea of tolerance. But the breakthrough was incomplete. Especially in Catholic schools, these historical events were mentioned only to be refuted. Youth was taught to obey and believe even when intelligence dictated otherwise.

This is one of the reasons why shortly after the turn of the nineteenth century the seeds of liberty could so easily be trampled down by the boots of fighting armies.

4. EVALUATION

If we now attempt to evaluate the bourgeois era in its entirety, we have to repeat our initial warning about the risk involved in such an enterprise. Every historical period is full of contrasts, overt as well as covert. And since, despite all efforts at objectivity, the later observer can never fully rid himself of the predilections of his environment and the bents in his personality, the picture he receives and gives of the past will never contain the complete truth. Every hero and every significant event of the past have been both praised and condemned, sometimes by the same critic.

Was Alexander the Great a ruthless adventurer, conqueror, and murderer of his most devoted friend, or was he the preparer of an empire in which the human races for the first time discovered their common heritage? Was Jesus the bringer of peace, or was he a rebellious radical? What were the Middle Ages: a period of the Christianization and unification of European culture, as Catholic historians believe; or an age of retardation and superstition, as the rationalists of the eighteenth century thought? There is some truth in each answer to each question. And how will our own present epoch stand before the judgment of future generations?

On the whole, the bourgeois was intensely human, with all the ambiguities which this word involves; half civilized and half barbaric, half progressive and half afraid of himself, half an idealist and half a cynic. He has been pitilessly censored by perfectionists, romantics, bohemians, and existentialists; yet, he was not worse than men of other periods. Indeed, his age was the most vital, vibrant, and productive one of all of Western history.

The *political system* of the bourgeois, though initially not undeserving of the Marxian reproach that it was the instrument of the rich for the exploitation of the poor, gradually adopted the principle of social justice. Incompletely, indeed. But the ideal state was a utopia even for Plato. Certainly, the bourgeois was all too willing to sacrifice the interests of humanity in the service of his idol, the nation-state: "My country, right or wrong." However, the increase of cultural exchange, the possibility of traveling without encountering a passport officer at every frontier, and the relatively free exchange of money, labor, and industrial products led the advanced countries further and further on the road of international communication. It was not amity but self-interest that brought people together. Less developed nations were mercilessly engulfed in the capitalist whirl and often suffered more than they profited. Nevertheless, the political and intellectual pales of feudalism were broken down, and enduring friendships developed among inhabitants of different countries. Considering the potentialities of progress from sectionalism to transnational relations, the outbreak of World War I and the insanity of the subsequent so-called peace treaties were catastrophes beyond description.

No doubt, the most characteristic feature of the bourgeois period was its *economy*. In its initial state, capitalist industry was fiercely acquisitive and irresponsible with regard to the suffering of the poor. But after the first period of unrestrained laissez faire, the chances of selling, buying, and saving created a higher level of prosperity than had ever existed. Contrary to Lenin's predictions, communism did not extend from precapitalist and largely illiterate Russia into the war-exhausted centers of capitalist enterprise. Even in the colonies, brutality slowly gave way to more humane management.

The *religious* life of the bourgeois was conventional, but there was something sound in this conventionality. It showed a growing distrust of the fanaticisms, the persecutions, and the psychic paroxysms of earlier periods. And there also appeared the most radical critics of superficial Christian conformism.

Also, the *humanism* of the time was more a habit of mind

than a profound experience; it was no longer the courageous humanism of the Renaissance and the Enlightenment. Unfortunately, under the impact of materialistic concepts of science it lost the metaphysical depth without which man's deeper understanding of himself is impossible. On the other hand, it was the bourgeois who transferred the theoretical ideas of the Enlightenment about the possibilities of human planning and progress into practical life. He changed the fatalistic and deterministic behavior of earlier generations into an attitude of rational courage and self-determination. Out of his ranks there rose a working humanitarianism that finally granted even the working classes the right to pursue happiness and self-respect. Women were increasingly allowed to participate in professional and public life. One discovered—perhaps reluctantly—that intellectually they were the equals of man.

Scholarship and the arts flowered, though the painters for whose works we now pay thousands of dollars starved. The typical bourgeois home was overstuffed with imitative furniture and bric-a-brac. No other century produced uglier government buildings, town halls, post offices, parvenu palaces, and factories. However, English and French architects experimented with new material, especially glass and iron, and before World War I three disciples of Berlin's Peter Behrens—Walter Gropius, Charles Le Corbusier, and Mies van der Rohe—began to change the architectural picture of our earth. But there were many others.

Finally, *education*, despite its antiquated content and its class character, in the secondary school of the bourgeois era an excellent preparation for higher studies in the most varied fields of scholarship was provided. Furthermore, school types of a more realistic and scientific character were founded, while at the same time the watermark of popular education was constantly rising. Certainly, the governments and the groups behind the schools used them to indoctrinate opinions and attitudes conducive to the preservation of their interests. But every vigorous and self-confident civilization will feel responsible for the transmission of its heritage, and the more it runs into a state of uncertainty, inner crises, and revolutions, the more it will court the soul of the younger generation. Nevertheless, there was less mind control and fear of differences of opinion in the schools of the bourgeois than in Communist countries and even in thousands of American schools.

It is, of course, a moot question to what degree schools aid genius or prevent it from flowering. Probably they do both. But if one counts the number of creative philosophers, theologians, mathematicians, scientists, poets, and musicians that appeared in the bourgeois era, then the schools of the bourgeois cannot have done so badly. Perhaps their very sternness helped to create rigorously struggling minds.

So far, we have omitted one criterion that helps much to reveal the character of a social class. That is its *sense of authenticity*, or its identification with values conducive to its genuine development. The authentic society, like an authentic person, has succeeded in directing its sometimes conflicting inclinations toward a durable equilibrium. Thus, we speak of the truly religious person, the true scholar, the true statesman, or the true artist.

Needless to say, in our complex society a lively human being relates himself not only to one, but to various, objectives. Indeed, he may become interested in so many things that he floats like a leaf on the currents of his environment and never arrives at "his truth," as Pestalozzi said in his "Evening Hour of an Hermit.[3] But men without their own truth are not the ones who impress their fellow men and contribute to the advancement of humanity. In the European societies, the nobleman, the priest, and the officer in the higher brackets of the army and the government were self-conscious and proud. They formed a clear image in the mind of the observer. Did the bourgeois achieve the same? To a degree, yes. There existed an image of the *Königliche Kaufmann* (the royal merchant) in the commercial centers of the West. He knew that the prestige, not only of his firm, but also of his country, depended on his reputation. But whereas the glitter of arms, the ministering of holy symbols, and the service

3. Part of this work is reprinted in Robert Ulich, *Three Thousand Years of Educational Wisdom* (Cambridge: Harvard University Press) [tenth printing], 1968, p. 480.

in the higher bureaucracy provided a transpersonal and firmly established focus of public respect, commercial enterprise did so to a lesser degree. Least of all did mere moneymaking. The rich parvenus and speculators, appearing in growing numbers as skillful utilizers of propitious market fluctuations, perhaps also of panics, certainly did not improve the image of the bourgeois, however much champagne they offered to their guests.

But now again, let us try another perspective. Neither in persons, and still less in social groups and whole countries, has the desire for self-identity been an unambiguous benefit. Often it has led to pride, arrogance, and exclusiveness. What the bourgeois society lacked in providing a clear image of itself, it compensated for in its mobility and openness to new impressions and experiments. Thus, it freed previously unreleased hopes and energies.

Unfortunately, the bourgeois was incapable of divorcing his political and commercial transactions from inherited nationalistic and militaristic conceptions of international life. He failed to free himself from the ancient human vices of greed and fear. Thus, he fed the fires of war rising under his feet and destroyed his great chances for progress from moral confusion to real civility. But while condemning him, we may ask ourselves: how far have we advanced?

Part II

The Years of Catastrophe

Chapter 3

THE STATE AND THE ECONOMY

1. THE STATE

For almost a hundred years after the defeat of Napoleon in 1815 the Western world enjoyed relative peace and security. Even such major military events as the Civil War in the United States and the Franco-German War did not gravely upset the political order. Hence, only a minority of Europeans realized the immensity of the impending catastrophe when in 1913 the clouds of war drew nearer and nearer. Military experts believed that the new weapons of destruction would make a protracted war impossible. They were surprised and ill equipped when the ex-pected mobility of action was replaced by the stubbornness of trench warfare.

Some peace-loving people, even from liberal and rightist parties, had secretly hoped that the growing Socialist move-ments would prevent open conflict, for the men in the factories might refuse to cooperate. Inded, after uncertain beginnings, the various Socialist groups of Europe had organized themselves in the Second International of 1896 and had waged an unrelent-ing war against the alliance of capitalism and militarism.

Some people also put their hopes in another international organization, the Catholic church, which, indeed, had severely opposed some nationalist and anticlerical governments, such as those of France, Italy, and Germany under Bismarck. However, when in 1914 the nations on the Continent found or felt threat-ened by an aggressor along, and even within their frontiers, the Socialist and the Catholic parties of every country voted for the war budget. Only a few brave individuals dissented. The great

French Socialist Jean Jaurès, who—caught in the desperate conflict between patriotism and love of peace, tried to avoid the disaster by an international labor conference—was assassinated by a fanatic driven to his act by the slander of chauvinists.

Reason and the grounds of Western civilization gave way, and the era of the bourgeois ended in the bloodbath of World War I. At the end of it, three empires—Russia, Austria, and Germany—the pillars of the old monarchical order, collapsed. Russia plunged into civil war, with the Bolsheviks emerging as victors; Austria was dismantled under the guise of the Wilsonian principle of national self-determination; and Germany was burdened with astronomical war reparations while trying to build a federated democracy out of religiously and politically divided territories.

Both Austria and the inexperienced German Republic exaggerated the idea of the right of minorities by introducing proportional representation, thus allowing insignificant and obtuse splinter groups to vote in favor of, or against, any coalition formed by the major parties, thereby precluding that essential element of all political planning: stability. The result was that the people, used to the old monarchical order, lost confidence in democracy as a system of government. They identified it with confusion, aimlessness, lack of decorum, and corruption. And if anything contributed to the general disillusionment, it was the failure of the United States to be true to the promise under which it had entered the war. Not without a sense of tragic failure can one read today Woodrow Wilson's "Fourteen Points," formulated in his address to the joint session of Congress on January 8, together with the address of February 11 on the "Four Principles," the "Four Ends" speech of July 4, and the "Five Particulars" speech of September 27, all in the year 1918. He demanded that the final settlement of the war be based on "essential justice" required by each particular case, that "peoples and provinces are not to be bartered about from sovereignty to sovereignty as if they were chattel or pawns in a game . . . that all well-defined national aspirations shall be accorded the utmost satisfaction that can be accorded them without introducing new or perpetuating old elements of discord," and that all nations "be

governed by the same principles of honour and of respect for the
common law of civilized society that govern the individual citizens of all modern States. . . ."

Finally, Wilson asked that all nations submit their special
interests, political and economic, to a League of Nations and
have no "leagues or alliances or special covenents and under-
standings within the general and common family of the League
of Nations."

In the peace treaties following the war, all these principles
were thrown aside or merely used as pretexts. The League of
Nations—planned by Wilson as a protection against divisional
nationalistic ambitions—became a covenant of convenanters unwilling to convene in a spirit of international cooperation. The
league was shackled from the beginning because the unholy
principle of absolute state sovereignty demanded that important
decisions be made only by unanimous vote—no nation should
be coerced against its will. The United States, which could have
given some strength to the new enterprise, was not a league
member because of the apathy of the people and the victory of
isolationism in Congress. Even before returning from Paris, Wilson had been betrayed by his secretary of state, Robert Lansing.
Nevertheless, the league took some steps in the direction of
international law and achieved some success in minor political
conflicts between nations willing to settle their disputes peace-
fully, as for example, between Sweden and Finland, or between
smaller nations such as Greece and Bulgaria, which could be
coerced by the bigger powers. The league was also able to agree
about some universally acknowledged humanitarian issues such
as aid to refugees, slave traffic, international health, and intellectual cooperation.

But in spite of the endeavors of some dedicated statesmen
such as Robert Cecil, the league became increasingly an instrument used by the more powerful countries for draping their
inertia or their egotistic decisions in the garments of legality.
The hopes for a new and peaceful world were frustrated by
narrow-minded politicians. They were largely responsible for the
moral crisis and cynicism of modern Western civilization. The
last luster of prestige disappeared when the member nations

failed to prevent a desperately overpopulated Japan from sever-
ing Manchuria from a defenseless China (1931) and when Mussolini was allowed to send his troops into Ethiopia in order to
divert the attention of his people from mismanagement at home
(1935). The assembled League of Nations listened politely to
Hitler's propaganda minister, Joseph Goebbels, who appeared in
Geneva to explain that the new totalitarian Germany was a
nobler and more dignified form of democracy than had ever
existed before. In 1937, Germany left the league.

A deep sense of guilt and disillusionment reigned over the
nations which thought they had won World War I. It created an
atmosphere of inertia that made it possible for the alliance between German national socialism and certain industrialist and
militaristic groups to build up the most threatening army of the
world. Whereas the Weimar Republic was never honored by the
visits of important foreign statesmen, they now paid their respects to the Austrian-born corporal who had become the führer
of the new empire of race hatred, class hatred, and hatred of
everything that had been considered decent and humane.

Seen in retrospect, the myopic attitude of the victors of
World War I with regard to the German situation borders on the
incredible. In spite of the warnings of men such as the English
economist John Maynard Keynes, the peace treaty, inflicted on
defeated Germany, created gigantic dimensions of inflation and,
when the inflation was over, of hunger and unemployment.
Many sympathized with France's desire to strike its eastern
neighbor from the world map. One failed to anticipate the
danger, which Lenin had already foreseen in his discussion with
the German moderate Socialist Kautsky, that after the breakdown of 1918 (for it was a breakdown and not a real revolution), the old reactionary powers of Germany would use the
despair of the people for their revival. Eighty per cent of the
German press was either outspokenly antidemocratic or luke-
warm in its defense. In the centers of administration the old-
cast officialdom reigned under untrained and mostly incapable
Socialist ministers. Many teachers in the secondary schools and
in the universities never missed a chance to remind their students of the "shame of Versailles" and helped spread the legend

that the glorious German army had been on the verge of final victory when it was "stabbed in the back" by peacemongers and mutinous soldiers. Crimes against the republic and the assassinations of leftist leaders were condoned. The murderers were not found. Hardly could the backward elements in the German government and in industry conceal their delight that Walter Rathenau, one of the greatest German thinkers and administrators of the postwar era, had been pierced by machine-gun bullets when on his way to the Foreign Office. As a Jew, so some thought, he should not have dared speak for Germany anyhow. In addition, he had advocated a better understanding of Russia's role in international politics.[1] This, of course, was "communism."

Even after the victory of Trotsky's soldiers over three "White armies," supported by Western powers but lacking in the most essential quality of a fighting army—an inspiring aim—the capitalist soldiers were certain that the economic system of the Bolsheviks would sooner or later collapse. When it survived, its opponents were reduced to moral indignation.[2] Everybody spoke about Russia, but respectable people sneered at those who uttered some words of understanding.

There were certainly reasons for repugnance. The Russian Revolution unleashed the centuries-old hatred of the suppressed peasants against their oppressors. The systematic organization of the "Red Terror" threatened the safety even of loyal comrades; its technique of inquisiton and torture rivaled the most demonic practices of earlier dictatorial powers; and its worldwide propaganda machinery clearly revealed the tendency toward world conquest.

But all these aspects of Communist Russia were no excuse for blindness concerning the causes of Russian revolutionary communism, its achievements in a situation of utter destruction, and

1. Harry Graf Kessler, *Walter Rathenau* (New York: Harcourt, Brace, 1930).

2. A good illustration of the long-lasting animosity against Soviet Russia, its diplomats, and their wives is in Ivan Maisky's *The Memoirs of a Soviet Ambasador* (London: Hutchinson, 1967). The author was Soviet ambassador to the United Kingdom from 1932 to 1943.

its success in changing a mostly illiterate nation into a nation
with an outstanding public school system. It was too easily forgotten that for more than a century Russia had produced a
galaxy of great thinkers and artists. Even during World War II
many advisers of Western governments were convinced that,
after the onslaught of Hitler's armies, Russia would have to be
grateful if the merciful allies lifted it gently from its tottering
knees. First at Yalta (February, 1945), where Churchill and
Roosevelt encountered the superior diplomat Stalin, and then
after the appearance of the Sputnik (October, 1957), the West
began to realize that the world of men had definitely changed.
Will the West make the same mistake concerning China and
Southeast Asia?

2. THE ECONOMY

As already indicated, prior to World War I Europeans and
Americans had an ambiguous attitude toward the state. On the
one hand, they were convinced, perhaps rightly, that the wheels
of industry and progress worked most smoothly when left alone
by the government and its bureaucracy. On the other hand, in
no way did they object to the help of the state in such unprofit-
able matters as education, welfare, and police. But there, they
believed, it should stop. Only Socialists and Communists—in
other words, the enemies of the nation—advocated a wider
interference of the state (which at the same time they intended
to abolish). When Socialists pointed to the fact that the government ran its post offices efficiently and that in many countries
the state-owned railroads were excellent and profitable institutions, the capitalist response was that they would work still
better if run by private enterprise. Anyhow, those institutions
were not "industries" or "producers" in the usual sense of the
terms.

Actually, the belief of the bourgeois that he could do everything just as well and even better without the state was a myth.
Just as a child wants to have his freedom and nevertheless ac-
cepts the shelter of his family, so also the bourgeois accepted
the protection of the state as a matter of course. After all, he

paid taxes, and he expected a decent return. Even the great captains of American enterprise, the most rugged of rugged individualists, who before 1900 paid no income taxes, wanted the federal army to protect the westward expansion of their private railroads. At the same time, the upper classes were offended when at the end of the nineteenth century the state refused to use its policemen and soldiers against such uncivilized activities as strikes and political processions. They also took it as self-evident that the government would stand behind the bankers by maintaining gold and silver standards and thus guarantee that the pound sterling, the dollar, the franc, and the mark would remain as reliable as the stars in the divine world order.

But then World War I completely subjected the life of man and his society to the demands of the hour. The first total war raged over the world. A person ceased to be a person; one's house ceased to be one's house; and the many strategic blunders of generals decided the life or death of hundreds of thousands. The governments, forced to abandon the standards of currency, entered the spiral inflation, especially those countries which for four and more years had been cut off from the world market. They could neither borrow the money they needed nor impose unbearable taxes on the citizenry. Had they done so they could not have kept up the "war enthusiasm" (*Kriegsbegeisterung*), partly created by patriotic fanaticism, and partly by the spurious impression of prosperity. For everybody—provided he could still work—suddenly earned more money; there was no unemployment, and the profits from the war spread from the big profiteers into larger segments of the population. Indeed, the few honest economists had difficulty in persuading even their learned colleagues that in the long run a country's prosperity was bound to suffer if the product of the people's work was not returned into the industrial process but shot into the air to arrive eventually in the bodies of young men. At the height of the inflation, the stamp of a letter in Germany, Austria, and other inflationary countries cost several million more than it had before the war; towns had to print artificial money to provide some means of exchange; and students who had gone into the mines in order to earn tuition could hardly buy a loaf of bread from their earnings.

Capital, pensions, and insurances evaporated. Humiliation, starvation, despair of any civil order, and mass unemployment caused the people to believe that it could not become worse than it was. Thus, in Germany they followed Hitler: it was better to march around in a brown uniform and protect the country against the "threat of communism" than to sit at home in the empty, cold kitchen and quarrel with one's wife. Dismissed officers and party leaders founded private armies in order to secure by might what they could not obtain by right. More and more, the situation resembled that of South Africa at its worst, or, to speak of the present, that of some African countries.

England, the Scandinavian nations, and the United States—the countries with an established party system and a long experience in the constructive interplay between the government and the opposition—escaped the continual changes of governments characteristic of other countries, including victorious France. But despite its internal disorder, France was still a model of tranquillity when seen against the continual revolts and local revolutions in the countries to the east and west of its borders. Even in the Anglo-Saxon and Scandinavian nations, the old order changed. Families that had contributed much to their country's culture could no longer keep up their style of living. The traditional class system did not disappear; inherited titles were still esteemed as a sentimental counterweight to the ever increasing power and prestige of money. But monarchs had to work together with labor cabinets; industrialists had to bargain with trade unions; and the state assumed more and more obligations, hitherto neglected or left to charity. "The country"—so said the embittered old bourgeois—"resembles a big welfare agency from which those profit most who contribute least."

Also the United States felt the lava of the volcano descending on its shores. Victorious and used to victory and to wide frontiers, it suddenly realized that there could no longer be real victories, for victories were followed by waves of moral and material depressions. Professors, having a deeper social conscience than they had actual experience with the real nature of either capitalism or communism, became Communist party members and taught their students the values of Marxism. It is little wonder that they went to extremes: they saw the much-praised democracies incapable of rescuing themselves and the world from the abyss of universal depression, unable to stimulate productivity and to secure employment for the millions of desperate people, and unable to arange the system of international debts and assets according to constructive financial principles.

One example may suffice to illustrate the helplessness even of highly esteemed economic experts in the face of the disaster of the early 1930s. In a publication of the Harvard Business School, the famous Professor Sumner H. Slichter ended his article, "The Adjustment to Instability," with the pessimistic statement that the modern means of regulating industry were so insufficient that chronic unemployment was inescapable.[3] Indeed, 40 percent of American out-of-school youth were jobless.

When finally the depression forced American financiers to withdraw their loans from the banks of Europe, while the victor nations of World War I tried to balance their floundering budgets by insisting on further payments from a materially and mentally exhausted Germany, the West was ripe for revolution. In view of the worldwide scale of the crisis and the inseparability of economics and politics, such a revolution was bound to assume international proportions. Hitler had to organize his military and social ventures by financial manipulations which inevitably led to conquest and the exploitation of other countries. It was not only political immaturity but also lack of economic understanding that plunged mankind into World War II.

3. *Business and Modern Society,* ed. Malcolm P. McNair and Howard T. Lewis (Cambridge: Harvard University Press, 1938).

Chapter 4

RELIGION, HUMANISM, AND EDUCATION

1. RELIGION

It has been an ancient privilege of priests to exorcise demons. There were enough of them in the first half of this century: warmongers, nationalists, racists, and dictators. In each battle the demons defeated the churches: Catholic, Protestant, and Orthodox.

One might understand the confusion of the Christian denominations at the beginning of World War I, for then diplomats and militarists had so muddled up the mind of Europe that every nation felt it had to defend itself against an aggressor. Under such circumstances the Church could use the old Roman concept of *bellum justum*, or "just war," which since early times Christians had welcomed as a means to assuage their bad conscience about organized human murder. Of such a war the Middle Ages had a shining example in the Crusades, although the motives behind the Crusades were by no means purely religious. The expeditions to the Holy Land had helped the ecclesiastical and secular princes to deflect political troubles at home into outward channels, and the crusading armies found unheard-of chances for commingling mystical devotion, heroism, brutality, and lust of conquest within an exciting venture, blessed by the church.

In using the concept of "just war," the clergy of 1914 was eagerly supported by patriotic philosophers, scholars, and, of course, businessmen. The few who dared to protest were ostracized as traitors and cowards. German nationalists excused even the invasion of neutral Belgium with the "law-transcending necessities of war." Unfortunately, they could point to the fact that a little more than a decade before the British had waged war against the Free South African Republic and had finally annexed it. England had no justification for moral indignation.

The real test of the strength came for the churches with the rise of the dictators Mussolini and Hitler. From Mussolini, the victor over internal troubles in Italy, whose henchmen had murdered the Socialist leader Giacomo Matteotti, the Curia accepted in 1929 the sovereignty of the newly created "City of the Vatican," ending thereby the fifty-nine-year conflict between the papacy and the Italian kingdom. The Supreme Pontiff used the occasion to praise the dictator's "exceptional statesmanship."

When, with methods the indignity of which was evident to the whole civilized world, Hitler had usurped power in Germany, Pope Pius XII concluded a concordant with the Nazi regime. Since the Catholic church is an international organization, with the pope claiming to speak *urbi et orbi*, the confusing effect of the concordat reached far beyond the German frontiers. The Curia also allowed the German bishops to sign, as early as in 1933, the Declaration of Fulda which practically delivered the German Catholics into the hands of the Nazi regime. Instead of setting Christian conviction against the pagan myth of the Third Reich, the church left it to the discretion of the individual Catholic whether or not he wanted to cooperate with the new regime. Nor did a later Fulda conference of the German bishops protest against the wars of aggression in 1939 and the following years; they only insisted on the rights of Catholic worship and other religious functions of the church in conquered countries and condemned, on the basis of the concordat, the medical experiments of the Nazi doctors such as sterilization and "mercy killing." Carl Amery, a pious Catholic, wrote in his widely read book *Die Kapitulation oder Deutscher Katholizismus Heute* (Capitulation or Today's German Catholicism): "Certain it is, and nothing can be said against this truth, that at least up to 1939, German Catholicism did do nothing for the protection of freedom of the Jews and the victims of the concentration camps." [1]

Also the Protestant churches showed no desire for Christian martyrdom. A goodly number of pastors supported the Nazi movement even more readily than the majority of the Catholic clergy. Nevertheless, the greater freedom and decentralization of Protestantism, while putting a heavier burden of decision on the individual congregations, allowed also for greater diversity. Whereas the pastors of the so-called *Deptsche Christen* (German Christians) used their rhetoric to persuade their congregations that national socialism (despite certain exaggerations, of course) was a movement of national liberation, true patriotism, restoration of moral purity, and German womanhood, the pastors of the *Bekennende Kirche* (the professing church), without any protection from above, risked their lives and told their anxious worshipers about the demoniacal character of Hitler's system. But like their equally courageons Catholic brethren, they were unable to persuade the hierarchy of the necessity of a radical stand against the enemies of civilization. What, then, were the reasons for the submission of such powerful organizations as the Catholic and Protestant churches?

However much the Catholic church may uphold the theory of its divine origin and the Protestant church may claim to be the guardian of man's individual conscience, both, like every other institution, depend on their milieu.

Especially with regard to the Catholic church, that milieu consisted of large strata of the lower middle classes, which had cruelly suffered from inflation and unemployment; thus, they discovered a kindred spirit in the would-be architect Adolf Hitler, whose mind overflowed with resentment against the more successful members of society.

1. Reinbeck: Rowohlt, 1963, p. 34. Two of the most inclusive books on the attitude of German Catholicism with regard to national socialism are Karlheinz Daschner, *Abermals Krähte der Hahn. Eine Kritische Kirchengeschichte von den Anfängen bis zu Pius II* (Stuttgart: Hans E. Günther, 1962), and Friedrich Heer, *Gottes Erste Liebe. Zweitausend Jahre Judentum und Christentum. Genesis des Oesterreichischen Katholiken Adolf Hitler* (Munich: Bechtle, 1967).

On the other side, the Catholic and Protestant establishments felt indebted to a patronizing aristocracy and bourgeoisie. Although thoroughly despising the shouting Austrian upstart, they welcomed him as an instrument for raising the nationalist spirit and for restoring "law and order." Foolishly, they failed to see that national socialism was essentially a movement of poverty and despair, that it was not at all interested in restoring a bankrupt monarchy and feudal form of capitalism.

Thus, as Carl Amery points out in his *Die Kapitulation*, the hierarchy had only two alternatives—either to form a heroic minority of Christians or to compromise with the prevailing political sentiment and thus to prevent its alienation from the German masses. The former course would have meant the separation of the church from the state under the protection of which, despite occasional conflicts, it had felt rather comfortable ever since it had accepted the authority of the government of Constantine the Great at the end of its prophetic period.

No doubt, ideological as well as political and financial motives influenced the hierarchy. During the nineteenth century and the first decades of the twentieth century, Christianity had been increasingly threatened by socialism and communism, by moral laxity, by the ideas of freedom and tolerance, and the skeptical rationalism of the Enlightenment. Were these not the very dangers which the new totalitarian leaders promised to abolish? In view of these possible gains, one had to pardon their racial hatred. Jews were not Christians anyhow. Many Catholics used the accusation of the Jews as the murderers of Christ as a legitimate excuse for anti-Semitism. They did not want to see that the blame of deicide (not refuted by the church until 1963 during the Second Ecumenical Council!) was one of the most inane myths under which mankind had ever suffered. For according to dogma, God decided in His infinite kindness to have His Son sacrificed for the salvation of mankind and chose the Jews as the executors of His will. How, then, could the Jews be blamed for an act for which every Christian should be infinitely grateful?

Perhaps, as many a bishop may have thought, with the victory of Germany over rationalist France and Communist atheism in the East, one could begin the religious reformation of rotten Europe and revive the medieval dream of a united Christian empire. Indeed, there were many profound and far-reaching questions to be considered by wise ecclesiastical statesmen who had lost the apostolic spirit.

Today, the new German Republic has many streets named in honor of those few simple citizens, students, scholars, and clergymen who were so deeply rooted in the message of Christ that even at the height of Hitler's power they preferred a lonely death to compromise. But who now speaks in Germany of the hundreds of young Social Democrats who resisted Hitler from the very beginning and were murdered in dark cellars right in the heart of Dresden and in other big cities? Is it because they were leftists, Socialist workers, perhaps Communists, and because most of them had left the church in which they could not longer honestly believe?

A last and very complex question arises: would all the martyrdom and the misery of the world have been necessary if the German Christian—with all his ancillary virtues of industry, obedience, and patriotism, and with all his piety, his Bible-reading, and his veneration of saints and shrines—had received that kind of rational and realistic education which would have enabled him to detect the fraud in Hitler before it was too late? Even a more embracing question may be asked, a question that is now more urgent than ever. Why were the modern revolutions in France, Russia, Spain, and Latin America anti-Catholic, if not antireligious, whereas the restorations and reactions, generally more cruel than the revolutions, were clerically supported? Was not national socialism itself a counterrevolution?

Thus, the problem emerges of the relation between authority and freedom in all its painful and never fully resolved polarity.[2] Man needs authority if he wishes to enjoy freedom, because freedom is empty without direction and purpose. But he also must be sufficiently free and independent to distinguish productive authority from self-seeking and misdirecting authority. He needs

2. See Paul Nash, *Authority and Freedom in Education* (New York: Wiley, 1966).

faith and confidence, but he also needs doubt and distrust. Where is the "right" boundary between the two?

No doubt, people subjected in youth to unyielding authority rarely become self-reliant and open-minded. Even when, generally under some violent conversion, they abandon old for new ideas, these ideas will be authoritarian in essence. Hitler, Goebbels, and other Nazi leaders were educated in the authoritarian fashion of older forms of discipline and Catholicism. Thus they were incapable of admitting the rightfulness of dissension. They had to found a new church and a new inquisition.

On the other hand, those who have never been able to believe and obey—although critically—will rarely grow into a life of mutual trust and cooperation. They are estranged not only from society but also from themselves, lonely in the crowd and bewildered when alone. Then families split, streets and parks become dangerous at night, and delinquency grows with growing prosperity and prolonged universal education.

One may criticize that this discussion of the religious problem in a world of confusion centered primarily on Germany. The reason is that the reign of Nazism not only changed the political aspect of the world but also provided a supreme opportunity for understanding the interrelation between political and religious powers. If similar situations arose in other countries, would the churches act differently? What have the North and South American churches done to combat the slavery and exploitation that have existed for hundreds of years? Only now, two decades after Hitler, young priests, pastors, and nuns join the protest marches of blacks and hungry migrants.

Now one last consideration. From a pragmatic point of view, and considering the power constellation in the empires of Mussolini and Hitler, the Catholic church acted prudently in avoiding a radical break. It gave comfort to the millions who were not bold enough to resist openly. One never prayed as much as under the yoke of Hitler. Although the church could not, as in medieval times, organize armies, it held out until, after a decade and a half, Italian and German totalitarianism collapsed. Without the Vatican, so we are told, Rome would have been chaos after the assassination of Mussolini.

Indeed, although during recent years established clericalism has been on the defensive, many Germans complain about the influence of clerics on the schools and their religious instruction, on political and academic appointments, and on radio and television. The churches are comfortable and tax supported, and teachers consider it wise to avoid the discussion of religious problems, even when the pupils ask for help. The frequent result among youth is cynicism. Unfortunately, this is not an exclusively German situation.

But the pragmatic test, so it appears, is not the only yardstick by which history and the human conscience measure an organization in times of distress. Eventually, in spite of his credulity and lack of knowledge (from which we all suffer) the "common man," as Lincoln called him, is a severe judge. Somewhere he expects cleanliness and salvation from the impurity of this world, and many have been taught to seek them in the Christian church. Even if this situation fails, it may survive for mere lack of something better. It will nevertheless be waning. All over the world people ask themselves how the church can claim to administer supernatural wisdom when it so easily wavers under the threat of demonic forces, intent on dividing mankind into masters and slaves, white and nonwhite, supermen and subhuman masses. At the Geneva World Conference of Church and Society, July, 1966, Professor Richard Shaull of Princeton Theological Seminary declared that "Christian existence is revolutionary existence." It should provide a context for revolutionary commitment and offer a theological perspective "for an ethic of revolution." [3] Christianity did so when its followers constituted a small and poor minority. But can the Christian churches—so intertwined and identified with the order of Western society—preach revolution?

2. HUMANISM

Early humanism was, at least in part, the expression of man's faith in his capacity to order his life according to norms he could

3. *New York Times, Geneva,* July 14, 1966.

find in his rational mind. This optimism, so vividly expressed by Hegel and Spencer, was shattered by the war, the peace that followed, and the rise of tyrannical systems of government.

Many humanists lost confidence. They retreated behind the cover of supernatural faith and became Christians of a sort, or devotees of Asiatic religions, or they turned to theosophy and anthropology. Others escaped the ever threatening attitude of despair through agnostic resignation, and some young men—not the worst—committed suicide.

Indeed, a sense of fin du siècle to the degree of cynicism had always smoldered under the layer of nineteenth-century conventionality. In France, Anatole France used his sometimes kind, sometimes cruel, satirical genius to reveal the corruption of the church and the governing classes. Even in England, a form of aestheticism was fashionable that effaced the distinction between right and wrong, love and lust, happiness and indulgence; Oscar Wilde is a prime example.

The country that up to the beginning of World War II preserved a more hopeful view of the human enterprise was the United States. It was due to that country's new sense of world power, mixed with residues of the old pioneer and frontier spirit, that in the periods between the wars and even later, John Dewey, the advocate of a humanist pragmatism, acquired a kind of popularity among his countrymen such as rarely, if ever, a living philosopher was allowed to enjoy. His most famous book —largely unread—*Democracy and Education*, became the bible of the American educator. It was appreciated as a patriotic manifesto of a democratic people involved in the fight against reactionary powers. Moreover, it expressed the spirit of a never defeated nation which—with all the signs of an incipient missionary complex of ever increasing magnitude—believed in its calling as the arbiter of a troubled world.

Finally, and with some understandable pride, the school of pragmatism was thought to be the first genuinely American contribution to the history of philosophy. Its origin can easily be traced back to Europe, though there it was regarded as "American materialism" in disguise, inferior to mature European culture and sophistication.

However, in his home country John Dewey had a calling. Following Charles S. Pierce and William James, he broke through the conventional type of European transcendentalism that had previously dominated the American departments of philosophy and education, and to an even larger degree in the country as a whole. Still today the observer of the North American culture will be surprised how much old-fashionedness reigns in this country of novelty, especially in religion—the general characteristic of immigrant societies in which a romantic nostalgia for the old and the pride of the new go side by side.

However, in the United States the incompleteness of pragmatism became obvious. Progress no longer seemed guaranteed by history, and the fruits expected from international experimentation and involvement did not ripen. To their surprise, the American citizens found themselves confronted with all the crises which in their buoyant mood they had considered the doubtful privilege of old Europe: financial upheavals, unemployment, rebellious minorities, even antidemocratic movements. They also suffered from a bad conscience: about poverty and injustice in their own midst, about the real causes of their participation in World War I, and about the peace treaties which had helped create World War II. Life was so much more complicated than it had seemed at the beginning of the century.

Thus, they began to understand that a philosophical system must be more than a theory of intelligent and successful behavior and that without an inherent cosmic element (which definitely was also in Dewey's mind but which for fear of metaphysical absolutes he never dared analyze comprehensibly), it is bound to remain on the surface. In order to be complete, a philosophy must be concerned not only with man as the creature that thinks and experiments but also with man that suffers, sins, and faces tragic realities. Here is the depth of the great religions. About this we will speak more in Part III of this book.

When Americans, dissatisfied with the shortcomings of pragmatism in a world of turmoil, looked toward Europe (from which in earlier times they had received their inspiration), they found little comfort and guidance. The old religions had lost their power over men who had seen their comrades bleeding in the trenches. Where was the benign and omnipotent God preached about from the pulpits? Why did he allow the slaughter of the best of the youth of so-called civilized nations? When the more educated men looked for help in the philosophy departments of the universities, they encountered professors with a sort of mental agoraphobia who did not dare liberate themselves from old speculative abstractions. There was no guidance for desperately searching humanity. Actually, never and nowhere has philosophy regained the role as the interpreter of the meaning of man and his history it had formerly played.

However, even before World War I, some professors had already left the barren grounds of academia and had concerned themselves with the immediacy of human experience, or with a "philosophy of life."

The most influential among them were the German, Wilhelm Dilthey and the Frenchman, Henri Bergson. As a result of his acquaintance with French positivist and English empirical thought, Dilthey had become skeptical of German Kantianism. He saw the purpose of philosophy as enriching the human mind by projecting itself into the actions and aspirations of the great exemplars of the human race. In this way, so he believed, would the individual transcend his personal limitations and vicariously participate in the events of creative history. Like William James, the author of the *Varieties of Religious Experience*, Dilthey developed to the finest degree the art of appreciating different types of personality and their modes of reacting to the challenge of life. Thus, he became one of the founders of modern philosophical anthropology and the theory of types.[4]

Because of his gift of *Einfühlung*, or of "feeling himself into" the multitude of possible positions, Dilthey ventured no finality of judgment, resignedly aware that one honest approach to the ever distant summit of truth may be just as valuable as another. The more deeply man searches into himself and the wonders of the cosmos, the greater will also be his awe before the final mystery of being. The great philosophical systems, or Weltanschauungen, are valuable in that they reflect the search and

4. See Martin Buber, *Between Man and Man* (New York: Macmillan, 1965).

thought of the best men of a specific period. They are nevertheless individual creations without any finality.

Although Dilthey's influence on modern thought was great and has constantly increased, he was at his time internationally less known than the French philosopher Henri Bergson. He too remained for most of his life a reverential agnostic, though before his death he leaned toward Catholicism. As in Dilthey, there was a strong aesthetic element in Bergson's thought. More productive than the traditional methods of scholarly inquiry, so he believed, is the power of intuition because it trajects man's mind into the creative center, or the *élan vital*, of cosmic life. This creative center must not be conceived of as something static, but as motion and change within eternal duration. The life of mind, as the life of nature, is a continuous striving; generalizations, therefore, are presumptuous. The dynamic character of Bergson's philosophy and the beauty of his style made him the spokesman of those who tried to combine a degree of relativism with a belief in some metaphysical direction, inherent in the depths of life.

Inevitably, the philosophies of Dilthey and similar thinkers, together with the cruel experiences of the world-war period, made thinking men skeptical about all preconceived abstractions, conscious or unconscious. What, then, could a person do but fall back on himself and engage with new intensity in the endeavor of unprejudiced self-scrutiny, even at the risk of abandoning formerly cherished beliefs which, so he now suspected, had perhaps more obscured than enlightened the situation of humanity in the world.

Far more than Dilthey, Bergson, and William James, three other thinkers helped modern man in this new search for self-knowledge—or, as one now says, in his "existential quest." Two of them, Kierkegaard and Nietzsche, had already died in the bourgeois period; the third, Freud, lived until the beginning of World War II. But his basic ideas also had their origin in the nineteenth century. All three, though admired by smaller groups, were fully appreciated only after World War I revealed to frightened man the bottomless tragedies lurking in human history.

The Danish theologian Soren Kierkegaard (1813-55) was for more than half a century the most neglected of all three, solitary and ridiculed while he was alive. The source of his profound psychological discernment was not psychology in the scientific sense of the term but ceaseless inquiry: "What is man in the eyes of God?" This question has tortured many great saints and theologians. It had led Saint Augustine, Luther, and the Jesuits to explorations into the depths of the human soul from which, despite all differences of standpoint, we still can profit.

Like Luther, an almost pathological personal involvement intensified Kierkegaard's religious concern. He lived on the borderline between illness and health, and like many who are socially unadaptable and afflicted with severe personal tensions, he was driven to probe with merciless fury into the subconscious depths and ambiguities of human life. He was opposed equally to the dubious compromises of bourgeois Protestantism, to super-stitious elements in the whole Christian tradition,[5] and especially to Hegel's, from his point of view arrogant, attempt to square the teaching of Jesus with the metaphysics of professors—though Hegel had probably no more skillful disciple in the art of dia-lectics than his opponent Kierkegaard. What, according to Kierkegaard, was Hegel's "World-Spirit" or "World-Mind" which, evolving within ever changing history and consequently unpredictable, had to employ such demons as Alexander the Great and Napoleon in order to push poor humanity forward? When would this World-Mind (essentially nothing but a product of philosophical speculation) arrive at its supposed ultimate goal —the unity of religion, art, and science? That which is itself a part of time can never reach into the eternal, for the eternal is *above* time, not merely its final fulfillment.

There is, according to Kierkegaard, no rational proof of Christianity. Man has to choose between Christ's radical de-mands on the one side, and, on the other side, his desire for a scientific and humanistic explanation of life—not to speak of his desire for material comfort. If he decides for worldly humanism,

5. See Herbert M. Garelick, *The Anti-Christianity of Kierkegaard. A Study of Concluding Unscientific Postscript* (The Hague: Martinus Nijhoff, 1969).

then he will sooner or later feel the emptiness which—according to Kierkegaard—inevitably arises in every life divorced from the divine source of strength and certainty. Thus, against modern scientific "objectivity," with its detachment from the concerns of the heart, Kierkegaard calls for "subjectivity" as a relentless search into the ultimate conditions of one's individuality. Here, all differences of Weltanschauung notwithstanding, is the bridge between the theologian Kierkegaard and the modern "existentialist." Both refuse cheap illusions and escapes from the predicaments of human reality.

In contrast to the theologian Kierkegaard, son of a farmer, the professor of classical philosophy Friedrich Nietzsche, son of a clergyman, argued against modern civilization from his deep immersion in the heroic, tragic, and Stoic thought of Greek-Roman antiquity. In his case also, a relation exists between ill health and thought. Only for a few years could he hold his chair at the University of Basel. But whereas for Kierkegaard suffering with Christ at the cross was essential to man's salvation, for Nietzsche Christianity was a subtle attempt of the weak to turn their slave morality into a victory over the strong. Kierkegaard demanded the courage of Christian surrender; Nietzsche demanded the courage of the superman.

No doubt, of these three thinkers, Freud has had the greatest influence on the modern mind. His analytical procedure has, so we think, taught us more about being human than Kierkegaard's emphasis on "subjectivity" (which really is not subjectivity at all but a variant of the old Christian fear of guilt before a threatening deity). We are also inclined to dismiss as a version of unrealistic individualism Nietzsche's Machiavellian idea of the existence of the few superhuman personalities who, though offending the customary standards of good and evil, represent the heroically productive element in human history. Unfortunately, the world fame of his profoundly beautiful *Thus Spake Zarathustra* has overshadowed such works as *Beyond Good and Evil* and the *Genealogy of Morals*, where he proves himself not only as one of the sharpest critics but also one of the wisest prophets of humanity. The fact that these prophecies were mostly of the Cassandra type makes them no less relevant and profound.

When reading Kierkegaard and Nietzsche, whose works abound with paradoxes (Kierkegaard's cerebration has been called "paradoxical theology"), one is himself inclined to use paradoxes. Both men, one could assert, have one characteristic in common: utter loneliness because of an intrepid and illusionless attempt at disclosing the hidden grounds in human motives —with the difference that Kierkegaard wrestled with the presence of God, whereas Nietzsche wrestled with his absence. And both belong to this fascinating group of thinkers whose very one-sidedness lead them into human depths hidden to the average mind.

Kierkegaard and Nietzsche were introspective thinkers. The influence of Freud, the third great modifier of modern man's self-understanding, is due to his empirical approach to the problems of humanity. It is now generally recognized that he might have interpreted the essence of art and religion differently had his outlook toward life not been molded at a time when philosophical and religious speculation was at the lowest ebb. As a scientist brought up in the second half of the nineteenth century, he was naturally inclined toward a form of materialist positivism to which our present scientists no longer entirely adhere. However, when one probes beyond his time-conditioned vocabulary and his one-sided emphasis on the role of libido and the Oedipus complex, one will discover that his concepts of the id, the ego, and the superego are but new versions of an old and probably perennial wisdom, expressed in other words by our great religious and idealistic philosophies. This wisdom says that the tensions in the human self (the ego) arise from its being suspended between a sphere of instincts (the id) and a vision of oughtness (the superego) and that a person matures to the degree to which he understands how to integrate the three spheres into a productive and self-mastering personal whole— an endless process, indeed, but the only one that makes life worth living. That which shocked the bourgeois was Freud's opinion—again not a really new one—that among all our so-called instincts the sexual is the most potent and, when suppressed, takes revenge and distorts the mental and physical health of the person.

If we now pass over from the forerunners of existentialism to existentialism proper, we should first keep in mind that none of its representatives likes the label. This aversion has deeper reasons. However much the existentialist thinker may be interested in the history of thought, he sees a certain arrogance in the philosopher's endeavor to catch the complexity of life in a system of logical categories. Rather, he understands the many tours and turns of philosophical speculation as the unceasing endeavor of man to clarify his relation to himself and the world as much as he is capable of doing *in his particular situation*. Existentialism is a way of analyzing humanity in man, passionately and dispassionately at the same time. It is, if one wants to say so, a certain form of self-conditioning that creates a specific inner attitude. Through a process of radical exposure, man is stripped of his sentimental fineries, false comforts, and inherited ideologies. He appears, as it were, in his existential nakedness. Or, if one likes a more positive phrase, the existentialist, doubtful of man's capacity to discover *the* truth, strives to discover *his* truth and to live an authentic life instead of one of conventionality.[6] (About a hundred years before the appearance of the existentialist movement the Swiss educator Johann Heinrich Pestalozzi declared it to be the goal of education to help a person to find "his truth," instead of subjecting him to the pressures and prejudices of his society.)

The earliest representative of the existentialist movement was Karl Jaspers, first a professor at the University of Heidelberg, then at the University of Basel. He initially developed his existentialist position on empirical grounds. As a physician he became interested in psychiatry and wrote a standard work in this field.[7] His observations led him to the conclusion that many

6. See especially Pestalozzi's "Evening Hour of an Hermit," in Robert Ulich, *Three Thousand Years of Educational Wisdom* (Cambridge: Harvard University Press [tenth printing]. 1968), pp. 480ff.

7. *Allgemeine Psychopathologie* (Berlin: Springer, 1913). American edition, *General Psychopathology* (University of Chicago Press, 1963).

problems of mentally disturbed persons resulted from inner up-
rootedness for which he found a partial explanation in Kierkegaard's diagnosis of the malaise of Western Christianity. Jaspers
was not only one of the sharpest critics of bourgeois confusion
between true progress and technological advancement (though
he offered no constructive solution); he also pointed at the unconscious bias in the great philosophical systems which so far
had dominated Western thought.[8] For however much their
authors believed that they had opened the doors to universal
truth, they never could completely free themselves of their own
subjectivity and its historical situation. Hence, the totality of
life will forever remain a mystery to men. We are within it and
feel it as an encompassing force (*das Umgreifende*), but its
essence, as Kant had already said, is veiled.

In his later and astoundingly comprehensive works, Jaspers
tried to escape the danger of relativism that despite all his asser-
tions to the contrary inhered in his thought by reaching deeply
—often in a tortuously individualistic language—into the problems of epistemology and metaphysics. These endeavors, however, did not prevent his remaining in contact with the events
of the time. In his recent book on the new West German Republic he again warned of the danger of superficiality that
accompanies prosperity. But, as always, he was stronger in criticism than in constructive and realistic suggestions.[9]

The dissolution of the older forms of metaphysics achieved
its climax in the work of Martin Heidegger, disciple of Edmund
Husserl, founder of the school of phenomenology. Heidegger is
the author of *Sein und Zeit* (Being and Time, 1927), probably
the most influential, though forever unfinished, book of modern
philosophical literature. Instead of using the conventional metaphysical categories by which older philosophers tried to explain
the order of the world, such as causality, growth and decay, or
good and evil—in the Christian tradition it was "God" as the
prime mover—the author of *Sein und Zeit* asks the radical ques-

8. Karl Jaspers, *Psychologie der Weltanschauungen* (Berlin: Springer,
1954).

9. *Wohin treibt die Bundesrepublik* (Munich: Piper, 1966). See also
Die Schuldfrage (Zurich: Artemis, 1946).

tions: Why is there something and not nothing? If there is being, what is its meaning? Is the Greek idea of *Logos* (which symbolizes the interaction of the human mind with the supposed inner order of the universe and as such has served as the conceptual basis of all Western philosophizing) perhaps nothing but a man-made construct, the result of his intellectual arrogance which demands answers even if there are none? Like the idea of God, the concept of *Logos* befogs more than clarifies our questions in the face of cosmic depth.

We may learn more about man when, without any preconceived ideas and illusions about ourselves, we analyze the tools which man employs, his behavior and moods in the precariousness of his existence, the care which he had to use in his struggle for survival, the sense of dread that permeates his life, and his reactions to the only certainty he has—the certainty of death. In some respects, our prelogical experiences may tell us more about human existence than our established scholarly vocabulary.

It is, therefore, no idle play with words that Jaspers and Heidegger anxiously scrutinize the rich, but also dangerous, potentialities of the German language. Indeed, the ever growing wealth and refinement of our experiences has enriched our language, but it has also revealed its limitations. Therefore, every poet and thinker is permanently struggling for new and original words. Even a hundred years before existentialism became a slogan, the French poets Baudelaire and Verlaine, to mention only two examples, shocked the French by the innovations of their style of writing (as well as by their style of living), just as much as the medieval nominalists shocked their contemporaries by their doubts about the efficacy of the human language to express the nature of God and His creation. One of Heidegger's early works deals with the nominalist Duns Scotus.[10]

However, when doubt in the trustworthiness of word and thought penetrates a whole period, it is always a sign of man's insecurity about his place in the universe of being and meaning.

In spite of their shortcomings, the philosophers of existentialism have had a most sobering effect on the easy superfi-

10. *Die Kategorien und die Bedeutungslehre des Duns Scotus* (Tübingen: J. Mohr, 1916).

cialities in the self-esteem of the bourgeois. But still greater and wider has been the influence of the existentialist novel. Man, so we learn there, may float happily on the river of conventions and fit himself nicely into his social ambience. But the quest for the meaning of his existence may never occur to him. A few are fortunate to find a vocation, a love, and a faith which help them over the hurdles and vicissitudes of the human career. Others may wander aimlessly in the labyrinth of delusions and illusions. As strangers in this world, they may, in all kindness and with a full desire for living, not really understand what is happening within and around them and accept even nonsense, if it helps them to survive, as do Kafka's and Camus's pilgrims on this mysterious planet. Or with Jean Paul Sartre, who has also gained repute as a philosophical writer, man, while looking at the crawling human vermin, may try to escape the feeling of disgust by taking a bold stand in the multitude of choices—though fully aware that the enemy's stand may be equally justified.

In the works of these writers (Hemingway could also be included), a certain type of modern intellectual believes he recognizes himself more clearly than in any other mirror. Indeed, not only the modern existentialist writers but also the great religious prophets have warned that intellectual arrogance may blind man just as much as sheer ignorance. And insofar as disillusion may create catharsis, existentialism has had a therapeutic effect.

But the mirror of the critics distorts the image. Were it wholly correct, humanity would have ended in a blind alley. No longer any vision of progress, but a question mark behind everything that man dares do and hope!

Yet, unprejudiced examination reveals to us also the greatness of man. Not only in the state of anxiety, boredom, loneliness, and expectation of death does he discover his deepest self. He discovers it also in love, heroic deeds, sacrifice, self-scrutiny, the courageous exploration of nature, and the many little duties of daily life: Man's future would be empty without the courage of faith and hope. And if, as Buddha teaches, life is but a series of delusions, let us choose those which give us the feeling that, in spite of all, it still has some inner force and purpose, even though death may be its only absolute certainty.

3. EDUCATION

How did education survive the turmoil of the wars?

In every country organizations arose which demanded that the sacrifices imposed upon the people, and on the working classes most of all, be rewarded by a total readjustment of the educational system. The access to higher forms of education should no longer be controlled by the social status and the money of parents but should be regulated according to the talent of the pupil. But probably the most impelling force behind the reform movement was the sense of moral indignation. How could old and proud civilizations murder each other for four or more years on battlefields, in civil wars, and, in a more subtle though not less cruel way, through blockades, starvation, enforced migrations, and so-called peace diplomacy? Apparently, the old moral and spiritual authorities had failed, especially the churches and the whole Christian tradition. What about all the official prayers for victory, streaming up to heaven from clergymen in their pulpits, from parents during their sleepless nights, and from mothers and children without a father in the house? If there were a God, must He not have been offended by invocations similar to those once offered to Yaweh, the Lord of Hosts in the Old Testament, ever ready to smite the enemy?

What had the humanities done to prevent the disaster? All the talk about the depth and beauty of the classical cultures, the great poets and the great philosophers, suddenly swept away; worse than that, just as in the Bible, it was converted into the rhetoric of hatred!

And all the highly praised discipline at home and in school! It had created nothing but obsequiousness, a desire for conformity and self-abandonment, a waiting for commands from outside because the inner voice had been silenced. Western civilization, so it seemed to the rebellious teachers and their friends, had become a big heap of hypocrisy. Its leaders believed neither in God nor in ideas, but in businessmen, generals, and disciplinarians. Herbert Spencer, the English philosopher, had already spoken of the pent-up desire for revenge on the part of the English colonial officers.[11] They maltreated the natives because they had been maltreated by the teachers of the fashionable schools of Eton and Harrow. Now the whole world had to pay for an inhuman kind of education.

In the ever swelling literature the term "the educational process" was preferred to the simple word "teaching," indicating thereby that henceforth one wished education to be an ongoing activity, a sharing of ever new experiences between teachings and pupils. Condemned to the limbo of dead or misleading values were such words as 'indoctrination" and "authority" (as if there ever had been a self-respecting society that did not believe in its right and duty to transmit its cherished values to the younger generation).

This depreciation of old values was not merely an affair of pedagogues and psychologists. It agreed with the conviction of many concerned men and women that the West was rapidly wearing away, as Oswald Spengler had said it would in his controversial *Decline of the West* (published in 1918, the last year of World War I).

The guide of the European progressive educator became Johann Heinrich Pestalozzi, who already about 1800 had asked for an "organic" form of education, though under the now abandoned aim of Christian piety. Now there spread from the United States John Dewey's educational pragmatism, also called "experimentalism," "instrumentalism," or "functionalism," the merits and demerits of which we have already discussed in the chapter on humanism. Geneva, the city of the League of Nations, became the home of the International Bureau of Education, while the international conferences of the "new Education Fellowship" provided the opportunity for progressive teachers to meet similarly minded men and women from other countries.

When in 1932 these teachers met in Nice, Hitler had already cast his shadow over the spirit of the assembly. Optimists were in the minority. Probably all teachers assembled at these reform conferences agreed on the necessity of a thorough change in the content and method of teaching. They dismissed the ancient

11. Herbert Spencer, *Education: Intellectual, Moral and Physical* (London, 1861).

languages as inert and wasteful; they wanted "schools for life" which made youth willing and eager to create a new social order. Few of the progressives envisaged the future role of mathematics and the sciences in modern life and teaching. A well-known theoretical physicist advised talented students to stay away from his field because they could not expect to get any positions. The new teachers had a low opinion of the applied scientists. These sciences—so they thought—were responsible for the materialistic trends in civilization. In addition, they had been the servants of the war industry. But one should not fight about the choice of subjects. Not *what* one learned, but *how* one learned, determined a young person's future. The school should cease to be "subject centered" and become "child centered."

Actually, there was nothing new in this conception. Aristotle had already anticipated it in his emphasis on the interest and involvement of the learner. Some medieval and Renaissance educators had criticized the harshness of the drill masters, and since the eighteenth century the battle for the rights of the child had been fought with increasing vigor. All the men engaged in this battle had acted under the impulse of general humanitarian principles and had condemned whipping and beating of children as much as inhuman laws and the maltreatment of prisoners. They recommended methods of teaching commensurate with the child's natural development; and they scorned the meaningless memorizing of the tricks of algebra; the irregular verbs of the ancient languages; the catechism; and the old-fashioned historical chronology, beginning with Moses, Solon, Lycurgus, and Numa Pompilius as the lawgivers of humanity.

Although the progressives were but a small and sometimes ridiculed group among the thousands of lethargic teachers, they came nevertheless at a time when the faith in the older educational methods had been shaken. They could no longer be ignored. Even conservative schools reexamined their curriculum, their rusty teaching habits, and their conceptions of the nature and capacity of the learner. Schools which today teach the same subjects by the same method as almost all schools did at the beginning of this century are backward. Only some of our college and university departments till old barren fields of learning with the old jagged plow.

However, the progressives wanted more than better schools. They wanted new schools because they wanted a new man in a new culture. And in this noble attempt they failed for several reasons.

First, for hundreds of years people had been convinced (and many are still today) that schools and teachers, even those in higher institutions, should leave public responsibilities to "more experienced" people. A politically active teacher was an anomaly looked upon with suspicion.

Second, teachers underestimated the tenacity of ingrained social conventions. At the time when Soviet Russia was building a threatening empire and a gigantic machine of propaganda, people critical of the Christian capitalist society easily became suspect of subversiveness. As has already been said, many of the reformers, returning from the horrors of the battlefields into physically and morally impoverished communities, were leaning toward communism. The French teachers' unions were dominated by it. Many teachers who entered public life could not leave entirely their classroom habits of abundant talking and expected the nation to listen to their superior wisdom. They thought both too much and too little about the power of words: too much, because inexperienced as they were in the ways of politics, they were impatient about the slow and recalcitrant acceptance of their ideas; too little, because they did not anticipate the irritation of parents whose children came home from schools with half-digested opinions about God, society, and the capitalist system—absolutely contrary to what father expected them to learn and to stand for when adult. Too many of those teachers who spoke of the "organic" development of the child were unaware of the conflicts in youths living in disagreement with their parents.

But did these teachers themselves—and here is the most salient reason for the progressive failure—have clear aims and policies? They rightly rejected rigid indoctrination in the name of freedom and wished to leave the dusty groves of obsolete traditions. But few people dare abandon known strongholds, even though they may be crumbling, without seeing new sign-posts for thought and action. The only ones, whether willing or coerced, who acquired a clear goal, were the Russian educators. They went through an initial period of progressive experimentation with some ties with the American progressives and with the German *Entschiedenew Schulreformer* (resolute school reformers), but they soon discovered that Western progressivism, despite its emphasis on a new community, was essentially individualistic. Russia's survival, they believed, depended on a rigorous coordination between the schools and the collective. Thus, after a few years of trial they constructed a school system, that, in full awareness of the value of efficient didactics, subjected the teacher and his pupils to the ideological discipline of the new society. With these methods they changed a largely illiterate mass into a well-trained modern society, the greatest world power together with the United States.

Part III

The Postwar Era and the Dawn
of the Idea of Mankind

Chapter 5

THE STATE AND THE ECONOMY

1. THE STATE

When recently—to use but one of many possible examples—the American Academy of Arts and Sciences arranged a seminar on the "Conditions of World Order," it invited just one philosopher among about twenty authorities on political, social, and economic theory.[1]

During the conference the humanistic interests of humankind were hardly touched upon, though one should think that in addition to politics and economics, they also contributed to the order (or the disorder) in which we live. The importance of religion was suggested mainly by non-Europeans. The other participants seemed to be inclined to relegate it to the somewhat obsolete and divisive sphere of metaphysics and ideology.* About education, the author of the *Conference Report*, Professor Stanley Hoffman from Harvard says: "The seminar's avoidance of the somewhat overwhelming subject of education in a 'monde fini,' despite Professors Malik's and Gadamer's references to its importance, is both understandable and symbolic" (p. 477).

1. "Conditions of World Order," *Daedalus, Journal of the American Academy of Arts and Sciences* (Spring, 1966).

* The term "ideology" was originally interpreted by Feuerbach, Marx, and other modern critics of society (with Machiavelli, Hobbes, and Spinoza as their forerunners) as a frozen set of ideas used by a dominating group to factitiously prevent the masses from recognizing their own interests. Today, the concept of ideology is often used for any one system of thought, apparently because we distrust all systems, even those with no other intention but to bring about a rational synthesis of ideas.

Indeed, the members of the conference reflected the common opinion of today. Ask experts and scholars alike which institution they hold most responsible for the future of mankind and they will name the state in cooperation with economics. The historical pressure evidently goes in the direction of state collectivization and centralization. As a matter of fact, the absolutist regimes of the predemocratic era, however cruel their interference in the individual freedom of their subjects, never thought of assuming obligations we now—even in the relatively decentralized United States—increasingly ally with the body politic, such as health, welfare, education, and large areas of commerce and industrial production. Since the citizen of today votes for his representatives in a parliament, he fallaciously believes himself to be a free participant and decision-maker in the affairs of his country and hesitates less to lay the management of his interests in the hands of the state.

Actually, the citizen never lived in a more ambiguous political situation. On the one hand, he emphasizes his individual freedom, security, and comfort. On the other hand, he delivers himself to a superindividual father figure, the future of whom depends on the behavior of similar father figures. No one knows, however, whether all these idols may suddenly be locked in deadly combat, with their soldiers no longer equipped with spears, swords, or old-fashioned cannon, but with atomic bombs and poisonous gas.

Hence men of all walks of life—statesmen, bankers, businessmen, trade-union leaders, scientists, and educators—assemble to found international organizations, from the United Nations and UNESCO to the hundreds of enterprises which connect experts of various countries for transnational action. For the first time in history men live in a worldwide neighborhood with a network of material and intellectual communications which, if brought to perfection, would initiate a new era of history. However, human fellowship comes about only when men are drawn together not by external forces but by mutual and voluntary obligations. Instead, the so-called peace in which we live today is upheld by the deterrents of "atomic taboo."

So far, the deterrent weapons—more global in their potential effect than any other human work—are controlled by two giant powers: the United States and Soviet Russia. Both hope that neither will outrun the other and thus yield to the temptation of exploiting its superiority. But they already look with suspicion at the rivalry of China and at the nuclear experiments begun by De Gaulle. And since inventions, first extremely complicated and expensive and therefore in the hands of a few, can in the course of time be more easily and less expensivly constructed, an increasing number of technically advanced nations will have the potential power of apocalyptic destruction in their arsenals. Furthermore, the still developing and therefore more nationalistic countries will be as eager to buy the coveted bomb as they now are to buy a computer.

If, then, through some accident or through the will of a desperate enemy, thermonuclear power is released, the whole carefully interlaced network of international balances and interactions will blow to pieces like a spider web in a hurricane. Because of this fear, the two superpowers are actually enchained in their own contrivances. A dwarf state such as Albania can play the naughty boy against big neighbor Russia and flirt with China, a very distant nation; Cuba's Castro brought the world to the brink of war; Formosa survives but a hundred miles away from continental China; Vietnam—small and corrupt at many places—has created a national moral crisis in the United States. A David may kill a Goliath. And many Davids, as they appear in the shape of small African and Asian states, may sometime band together and throw their weight toward one or the other of the big rivals. Despite their present weakness and dissension, they may form a wedge between the West and the East, skillfully using the situation of international rivalry for deals in food, armaments, and industrial aid.

Never have so many lawyers been so busy writing constitutions, so many diplomats and international jurists wrestling with frontier disputes, commercial contracts, maritime and fishery rights, and matters of communication, only to learn a few years later that the proposed measures have created new and even more imperious problems. Yet it is still better to reason than to fight. Despite all disappointments, we should acknowledge the merits of the various Hague conferences and The Hague Court of Arbitration, the League of Nations Court of Permanent Justice, and the work of the United Nations. And although, as a result of the disastrous Vietnam war, the international prestige of the United States has dwindled, we should not forget how much it has done to stem Communist aggressiveness in various parts of the world, and in Germany through the Airlift and Marshall Plan.

Unfortunately, in contrast with civil law, there exists in the international field no sovereign power to enforce peace and order—only hundreds of international treaties and solemn avowals concerning mutual security and the rights of men and nations. It is as with the Ten Commandments: everybody holds them in great respect, but they have never tamed the brutishness in man. In earlier times also, powers great and small preferred might to right and disrespected the agreements to which they had subscribed. Yet, the fragile virtue of international conscience was perhaps stronger in past centuries when under the influence of the Dutchman Hugo Grotius and his successors, personal and international law were interpreted as the reflection of the "natural order" inherent in the divine universe. This sanction has been destroyed by modern relativism, historicism, and positivism, according to which law derives merely from agreement among partners and consequently changes with their interests.

How peaceful appears to us the century between the defeat of Napoleon and World War I! At least some statesmen of that period succeeded in concluding treaties that were more than simply a continuation of war under different auspices. These statesmen belonged to an aristocracy that spoke various languages and served monarchs belonging to internationally related families, with no interest in destroying their own prestige by destroying the monarchies of other countries. Contrary to prevailing opinion, democracies—dependent on political leaders whose popularity and reelection depends on shifting majorities—are more easily the victims of the furies of mass instincts than were regimes rooted in monarchical traditions.

Nor should we indulge in the hope that as a consequence of

increased global interdependence the citizens of today are less nationalistically minded than the patriots of earlier times. The nation-state with all its self-exaltations on the one hand, and its fears on the other, is not dead, as some of us would like to believe when reflecting on its inadequacy, just as the churches are not dead because one would prefer a better answer to the spiritual quest of modern man.

If we had freed ourselves from the grip of the tribal anxieties of barbaric ages, we would have stopped the madness of the modern arms race, as it is exposed by a report of the Stockholm International Peace Research Institute of the year 1969. According to this report, the military budget for the world doubles every fifteen years. In 1968 the world spent $159.3 billion for military purposes, with the United States as the largest spender ($79.3 billion), followed by the Soviet Union (officially $39.8 billion, but probably considerably more). More than 70 percent of the world's total costs for armaments were spent by the United States and the Soviet Union.

As Gunnar Myrdal has explained in his book *Beyond the Welfare State*,[2] the increase in the care of governments for the well-being and education of their citizens has actually attached them more to the national regime than was the case in times of greater decentralization. Any alleged danger to security immediately creates mass anxieties, and if the danger comes from abroad, it will be answered by fear and cries for increased armament.

However, the discrepancy between the order we should have and the disorder in which we live should not allow us to submit to radical despair and to the belief that we are mentally and morally inferior to our ancestors. The political currents they had to master, or failed to master, were feeble in comparison with the tides of modern history. Up to the nineteenth century, almost all major decisions were made in Europe and, to a lesser degree, in the United States. The other continents were merely objects with little chance for successful rebellion. Although the mighty were always divided by contrasting interests, their di-

2. New Haven: Yale University Press, 1960.

visions were not yet intensified by the conflict between capitalism and communism.

These, then, are the tasks which the leaders of the world and we all will have to master!

First, we have to learn the difference between patriotism, or national loyalty, and nationalism as a chauvinistic attitude. After the foregoing discussion, this difference is evident. It should be the privilege of every self-respecting man to belong to a politically identifiable unit that protects his safety and his freedom. This belonging expresses itself in patriotism. Nationalism, on the other hand, grows from a person's excessive identification with his group at the expense of all other responsibilities necessary for a sound international equilibrium.

Nationalist sentiments inevitably increase in times of danger. They grow with the sense of injustice and frustration. Hence, defeated and humiliated peoples, still struggling for national purpose and coherence, such as the newly emerging states of Africa and Asia, are the most belligerent and easily offended carriers of the nationalist bacillus. Nevertheless, the most shameful record of political irrationality—morally equivalent to the burnings of heretics and to the witch trials of earlier times—has been the frequent mistreatment of ethnic minorities in countries small and large. In order to get rid of these minorities and at the same time a bad conscience about their unjust treatment, during the past decades the so-called civilized nations have resorted to ancient barbaric means of mass annihilation and enforced emigration. They have hit Armenians and Greeks, Germans and Poles, Hungarians and Arabs. The history of the Jews and of the blacks, of course, is the most awesome illustration of human fear, bigotry, and cruel fanaticism. But we should now understand that hatred engenders hatred and at the same time a permanent feeling of anxiety in the victor. As the early Negro leader Booker T. Washington said: "You cannot hold a fellow down in the ditch without going down with him."

And for the new struggling nations, so we should have learned, there exists no other way toward global peace but that the nations with a settled political tradition abandon their moralistic, hypocritical and protective arrogance, exercise the art of forebearance, offer their help, and try to direct their boiling energy into productive channels. Nothing is more harmful to sound international development than the endeavor of more powerful nations, however well intentioned, to impose their supposedly superior order of living on countries still struggling for their identity. In that way they cripple their organic growth and achieve exactly the same result as with the suppression of a young person's strife for independence; namely, resentment and rebellion. Even economic assistance will not change the mental picture. Pocketmoney does not always make good children. In this respect, the statesmen of the United States have made one blunder after another, often with the best intentions, and for these blunders this nation is paying dearly.

The second problem that must be faced is the conflict between the democratic and Communist conceptions of government. The contrast is, often very glibly, indicated by the ideological polarities between "free," "liberty-loving," and "Christian" nations on the one side, and "totalitarian," "materialistic," and "atheist" nations on the other.

There is some truth in each of these phrases. Whoever has lived under a totalitarian system and has lost the "inalienable rights of man," such as *habeas corpus* and freedom of speech and assembly, will know what this loss means to a self-respecting person. These values are taken for granted by the American citizen (at least as long as he is not confronted with the problems of segregation, race riots, antiwar marches, and student rebellions). But he should project himself more often into the situation of citizens of foreign countries, whose authors are taken to prison; whose borders are guarded by high walls, barbed wire, guns, and police dogs; and whose homes are invaded if they dare deviate from the policy of the master nation. He should ask himself what this perpetual humiliation of humanity means ultimately to each of us.

There is an essential difference between those nations in captivity which have behind them a long political and cultural tradition with a degree of freedom, however variously interrupted, such as East Germany and Czechoslovakia, and those large segments of mankind which suddenly pass from a state of mass poverty and tribal anarchy, or from colonial dependence and the rule of foreign administrators, into a state of sovereignty without adequate political preparation. The former would know how to rule themselves, as did West Germany after its liberation from Hitler; whereas the latter can maintain a minimum of stability only by centralization of power wielded by a strong man with the help of an army. Even in so-called free countries the power of the military increases almost constantly.

The Western nations, too, went through some kind of totalitarianism, though of a feudal character, before they created the conditions of democracy. These conditions were not brought about by rational planning. Rather, they evolved from city life, commerce, communication, technology, and enlightenment— which Russia before 1917 had only in small measure, and which the newly emerging nations from Egypt to central and southern Africa and in large parts of Asia did not have at all, despite great spiritual and aesthetic riches.

The gap between the totalitarian and the nontotalitarian world can narrow only if the increase of wealth, together with the demand for more freedom of thought and action, will force the Communist leaders and theoreticians to loosen the reins of dogma. The neo-Marxists such as Ernst Bloch, Georg Lukács, and Karl Korsch have already emphasized that the Marxian doctrine of evolution itself implies social and ideological changes. The truth of this assumption is evident from the ever growing unrest in the Communist camp. Marx himself never was a "Marxist."

While the more advanced Communist countries are struggling for some compromise between authoritarianism and personal freedom, the capitalist countries are increasingly forced into measures of centralization and control, totally unexpected at the beginning of this century. For only through such measures, welcome or not, can they lead the citizenry through the turbulent and muddy water of modern life. About this we shall see more in the following chapter on economics.

But if we want the advantages of governmental surveillance and support harmonized with the value of individuality (still best, though imperfectly represented by democracy), let us constantly keep in mind the dangers of the two extremes. On the one hand, excessive individualism has often created the very opposite of democracy: namely, the exploitation of the many by the favored few, contempt of the common concerns of mankind by intellectuals and aesthetic snobs, and an educational system in which wealth and caste went before talent. On the other hand, planned management from above tends to pull increasingly large segments of the total life of the citizen into its orbit, to make the individual person a member of a gray collective, and to dull his sense of personal initiative and responsibility. Too much security can become an invitation to idleness, even to criminality. Even for the indigent, knowledge of the nearest welfare agency has not always been a blessing. Just as power corrupts, so may indiscriminate reliance on outside help. When listening to politicians who before election and reelection promise to provide a carefree life for everybody, we should not forget how much the seekers of influence in the later Roman Empire contributed to its decay by promising the masses *panem et circenses*—bread and amusement.

Closely related to the collectivist-democratic antinomy is the *third* task of present statesmen. This is to create a sound *balance between political consensus and dissension*. Under the disguise of democracy, certain politicians, who are totalitarians at heart, frighten the people into a state of mind where they see an enemy in every dissenter among their own people, and a threat to national existence in every disagreement with a foreign country. Fear, herd instincts, and their sinister companion, aggressiveness, have always been the foredoom of disaster. Every tyrant has risen to power by creating an atmosphere of catastrophe while at the same time promising richer and morally superior ways of living. Italy had Mussolini; Germany had Hitler; and the United States suffered the miniature edition in Joe McCarthy. When one surveys the present political situation, he will find that dogmatism and absolutism are more frequent attitudes than liberalism and tolerance. The simplistic answers of the former are more easily accepted by lazy minds than the balanced opinions of thoughtful men.

The fourth hurdle on the road to democracy, and through it

to mankind, is the *racial problem*. Hardly any social dilemma is so laden with hostility, stubborn prejudice, unrealistic sentimentality, and a sense of helplessness. The predicament is especially grave in the United States, where after centuries of oppression the large black population refuses to live any longer on the bottom of a hypocritical society. At the same time, for lack of education and chances for constructive initiative, many blacks are insufficiently prepared for the uphill struggle. Prudent leaders then lose control easily over the impatient, who advocate violence as a shortcut to progress and as revenge for the violence suffered in a cruel past. And wherever there is rioting, hungry people may fall to the temptation to steal food and clothing from a neighboring store, while the criminal element thrives on the disorder, looting, and alienating even those predisposed to support the cause of the poor.

Even the South American nations, generally known for racial intermarriage, discriminate. The higher strata of society are more prejudiced by color of the skin than the bulk of the people who judge their neighbors primarily in terms of income, education, and modes of living.

On the whole, intense racial consciousness seems to be the doubtful privilege of the Germanic populations, though, fortunately, the offspring of mixed marriages between white women and black soldiers during the German and other occupations after the wars have been tolerably integrated. With the improvement of the schools for the black it has become evident that there is no such thing as an "inborn" trait, a term which, as an excuse for inactivity, has always belonged to the pet vocabulary of racially and socially prejudiced groups. Man, so they preached, should not change what "God," "nature," "instinct," or sacred traditions have ordained to be in the order of the universe. Therefore, serfs in old Russia had to be kept illiterate; the peasants, if lucky, in Western Europe had to be satisfied with a minimum of schooling; and before the Civil War, several Southern states of America made it a crime for slaves to read and write.

The Middle Ages, so it seems, did not have our form of racial discrimination. Until the Crusades and the Inquisition the Jews were tolerated and exploited no more than other powerless groups of the population, and one fought the Arabs not because they had a differently colored skin but because they were followers of the devil Mohammed and occupied the Holy Land. The medieval Black Madonna of Czestochowa (not the only black Madonna in the East) still attracts more Poles at ecclesiastical holidays than the Communist government can muster for its national processions.

Children from unprejudiced homes are not color conscious until they go to school. The American child, whether white or black, is aware that his future will be influenced by the race and class of his parents.[3] It seems that with sexual maturation, racial awareness increases in the majority of young people, augmenting that polarity between aversion and attraction that is characteristic of erotic relations.

Furthermore, we all are children of habit. With growing integration of mixed couples into the totality of the population, the feeling of otherness may gradually fade. However, it will take a long time. For the race and color problem grows out of and inextricable compound of cultural and psychological factors, shot through with long established prejudice and sanctimony. And here is the danger. Kant called prejudice a form of judgment that refuses to correct itself. Thus, like nationalism, it cannot be abolished by mere force. Unwilling people react to imposition either in forms of violence or of hypocrisy and subterfuge; both undermine the moral fiber and inner coherence of a nation. Education, persuasion through enlightened ideas, and factual proof are necessary to change the minds of the recalcitrant. Time, reason, and demonstration, as history has often shown, may still defeat some of the demons of darkness.

On the other hand, let the white citizen not be bowled over by those who respond to any attempt at racial reconciliation with the question: "Would you like your daughter to be married to a Negro?" This is not merely a problem of color. Many black families are as little fond of interracial marriages as are whites.

3. See Robert Coles, "Northern Children under Desegregation." Report read at the 123rd annual meeting of the American Psychiatric Association, Detroit, May 12, 1967.

Neither wish their children to be exposed to cruel social ambiguities which even strong human beings rarely suffer without
inner damage. They may be capable of wrestling a weapon out
of the hands of an enemy, but they cannot blunt all the arrows
shot at them by the bows of malice and social hatred. Doubtless,
also, the desire of parents to preserve their own image of social
prestige is a powerful factor in the objection to interracial
marriage.

But how much would we gain if each citizen of the United
States could say in complete honesty that, as a professor, he
would be glad to work under a black president; as a business
man or banker, under a black executive; and as a trade unionist,
under a black boss. Yet, let us not deceive ourselves. If by some
historical quirk in certain regions of the South a sovereign government appeared and, like the Hitler regime, decreed racial
violence by law—heaven knows how many fires would suddenly
burn on roads which people hoped to tread in safety! Unfortunately, the problem is international and will intensify because
of the rising immigration of poor people from underdeveloped
countries into the more fortunate industrial centers with a generally more educated population.

It may not *always* be racial prejudice but rather defense of
standards of living that render people hostile to the sudden
influx of foreign groups—both unprepared to meet the other.
A deep murmur of discontent and danger can be felt wherever
too different groups come too close to each other. The white in
South Africa and Rhodesia claim that they protect not only
their property but also their culture. At the same time, they
fear what will happen if the fury of the black man is released.
The Chinese no longer feel safe in Indonesia. The White Russians are uncomfortable in Manchuria, which for centuries
belonged to the great empire of the Manchus. And white inhabitants of New York would be more foolish than ever to
venture at night into certain streets of Harlem. Some white men,
even unconsciously—and that might be worse because it proves
the depth of the roots of prejudice—commit by use of careless
language irreparable cruelty to black children, there endanger-

ing the hoped-for unity of their nation, for a soul intensely hurt in childhood does not easily forget.

Nevertheless, during the past decade the society of the United States has made surprising strides toward equality under the law. Blacks are selected for important public offices. A black professor has been appointed president of Michigan State University. Riots are not merely rejected with righteous indignation or by police forces. Increasingly, people try to understand them and to correct their causes. In spite of all resistance, more and more young men and women with high social and educational backgrounds are breaking through the color barriers.

Second, in order to acquire the necessary degree of calm self-assurance, the black must be given hope that his efforts at successful competition with the white will bear fruit. If the first years of schooling, often occurring in an unhealthy environment, prove to him that the conditions of his often-changing home and the ensuing limitations of experience and language put him automatically into the lowest group of students, he is likely to become a high school dropout. (European educators have discovered that few children of workers attend advanced schools because of their early difficulties in expressing themselves adequately.) Therefore, we need in schools that have a high percentage of black and Puerto Rican children methods of teaching that supplant the old forms of teaching and grading with an elastic and individualistic curriculum. Certainly, much of the burden of making our society a society of hope falls on the elementary schools.

A look into the past may contain some encouragement for the future. The great Swiss poet Gottfried Keller tells us in his novels that almost up to the middle of the nineteenth century the lower-class Swiss was subjected to the most humiliating forms of jurisdiction. In some city-states, the children of peasants were expected to kneel on the street when the landlord, most of the time living in his urban home, visited his estate. Switzerland, as all Western European nations, still carries signs of the old class structure. Nevertheless, it is now rightly admired as a model of republican freedom and justice.

However, the two main factors in the process of integration will be, first, within a pluralistic society dominated by the white, the black must be capable of finding his identity. As with every person, whether young or old, who has been shaken out of his natural self-assurance, this finding of one's self goes through ups and downs, through excessive ostentation mixed with excessive frustration, through phases of impatient arrogance and phases of demureness. But certainly the compromising attitude of the ex-slave Booker T. Washington, the founder of Alabama's Institute for Negroes, belongs to the past. Already in his lifetime it was rejected by the first Negro Ph.D. from Harvard, William E. B. Du Bois; by John Hope, president of Atlanta University; and by other black fighters for racial equality.

Notwithstanding all the disturbing extremes between the "Dark Continent" and the industrialized nations, Africa has changed within the past decades. All over the world, separateness will more and more become a political and economic impossibility. The daily press, books, and television tell us about the life of people on the five continents. If governments (which are sometimes behind, but sometimes ahead of the population) exercise a consistent influence upon stubborn minds, the coming generations will no longer see a sign of inferiority or threat in foreignness, but a challenge and, in many cases, a chance of enrichment.

Probably the most difficult task of the statesmen of the future will be the control of the population. A teeming mass of humanity, fighting for its very life like vermin on a corpse, cannot achieve peace and unity. Out of sheer hunger, inevitably combined with aggressiveness, irritation, and irrationality, men will create situations which frustrate every effort to combine individuality and dignity with the spirit of cooperation. Through polluting the air, water, and soil, through increasing exhaustion of the already dwindling resources of the planet, mankind will turn the blessing of fertility that so far has made possible the survival of the species into the curse of self-destruction.

With respect to the United States, after three centuries of population growth, one hundred million was reached by 1917.

Fifty years later the population was two hundred million; at the present rate of growth it will be three hundred million by the end of the century.

By some means, Americans may survive. But what about the total population of the earth? It reached one billion in 1830—which already was far beyond anyone's expectation at the time of the Reformation. It climbed to two billion in 1930. Provided this growth continues, the earth's population will reach seven billion at the end of the century. Thereafter, an additional one billion would be added every five years.

Tragically, Pope Paul VI, allegedly speaking with divine authority, threatens with eternal punishment those Catholics who, for various reasons, practice artificial methods of birth control.

The discussion of the five tasks of modern democratic statesmen, namely, to clarify the relation between patriotism and nationalism, between liberty and totalitarianism, between consensus and dissension, the solution of the race problem, and finally the control of the growth of population, forces us into an examination of the real significance of the two concepts of democracy and communism. What do they really mean in our time? Do we perhaps use a vocabulary that has changed its substance within the past decades?

During the nineteenth century, the term "democracy" carried a dubious, if not negative connotation in many countries. In monarchical Europe, the term "democracy," adopted by sixteenth-century thinkers from Greek political theory, provoked an uncomfortable feeling among the ruling classes. It might have been all right in the faraway Athens of Pericles, but at the present it suggested such subversive ideas as equal rights vested in the people without any differences of rank and money and without respect for the divinely established social hierarchy. In the Revolution of 1789 the French used the term *démocratique* in opposition to *aristocratique*. Hence democracy smacked of barricades and of the reign of the street and of the guillotine. A man with such a serious attempt at objectivity as the aristocrat Tocqueville, author of *De la Démocratie en Amérique*

(1835 and 1840), warned Europe against the dangers of a political system in which liberty (which he cherished) would finally succumb to colorless equality (which he hated).

After having been accepted into the established order, the bourgeois agreed with the conservative critics, for he was afraid of agitators who made the workers restive and asked questions about franchise and decent payment. Some enlightened bourgeois might not have minded being called liberal; they may even have espoused republican ideas, as did many antimonarchical Frenchmen. But on the whole, they were not democrats.

Furthermore, in France—politically the most troubled country on the Continent—there was an outspoken suspicion that the statesmen of the democratic regimes were not persons of high moral quality but were egotistic politicians and demagogues who professed their love for the people but cooperated secretly with sinister speculators. The novelist Anatole France was certainly a liberal man, but he distrusted the democrats at least as much as the aristocrats. Today the French, and certainly also the German grocers in a small town, feel honored to serve a countess even if she is late in paying her bill.

Not before the second half of the nineteenth century did the more advanced European nations gradually introduce democratic institutions such as universal suffrage. But the democratization was incomplete. In Germany, the higher positions of the army and in the diplomatic service were generally reserved for the nobility. Not before 1916, that is, in the middle of a war, with the sons of the nation fighting in the trenches, did England have its first prime minister from the lower classes, Lloyd George.

Even in the United States—the pattern of a "free country"— people were not altogether united behind the word "democracy." Until the time of Jackson, who became president in 1829, this country was governed by the upper classes. It took about a decade after Jackson, and, of course, much more time in the South, before, as the phrase went, the people "governed itself."

Certainly, for their time the Founding Fathers were revolutionary thinkers, acting in the best spirit of the Enlightenment. They dared oppose the myth of the divine right of kings, of one group riding in the saddle and the other holding the stirrups, and of the unworthiness of practical work for the gentleman. They also had, at least in part, a bad conscience about slavery and intended to abolish it. But though they were called rebels by the English, the large planters of the South and the merchant capitalists of the North were essentially conservative and property conscious. They were intensely concerned with preventing the fight for liberation from running into political and religious extremes, as the French Revolution did but a decade later.

From Americans born about 1880 one could hear that in their schools they never heard of living in a democracy. They were told they lived in a republic. Only during World War I (when the oath of allegiance was introduced to the public schools) did the term "democracy" become popular as a convenient means of propaganda. The war was fought with the slogan "to make the world safe for democracy." Even so, men of "quality" were not altogether happy. With the rapid urbanization and industrialization, especially after the Civil War, money and external success had too one-sidedly become the criteria of worth. Things were no longer done for their inherent value; rather one asked how much they were worth. The ends justified the means.

During the first half of this century, the novelist and social critic Edmund Wilson, certainly one-sided in many respects, but perceptive and, at times, profound, distinguished between true republican idealism or the spirit of the republican Roman on the one hand, and the new form of materialist democracy on the other. The first, so he thought, disappeared at the end of the nineteenth century and with it that sense of true human equality which had made every honest and responsible man, whether rich or poor, essentially equal to any other. Instead, so Wilson says, the nation became divided into a class of the rich, money-grabbing and railroad-building entrepreneurs, and an increasingly undifferentiated mass, both groups equally contemptuous of culture, and vulgar in taste. According to Wilson, there also appeared a monolithic state, no longer run by statesmen such as Lincoln but by men who gave a bad odor to the once-honored word, politician.

After 1918, the "lost generation" searched in vain for political ideals. Today, frightened by the terrors of tyrannical systems in Europe, the typical American has ceased to be a progressive and courageous republican, proud of a revolutionary tradition; he has become more and more a supporter of reactionary governments, thus preventing developing and suppressed nations from going through their own inevitable revolutions. Whenever a poor nation fought a dictator who sympathized with capitalism, the American government protected him. Indeed, such is today the reputation of "freedom-loving" America that it is difficult to convince foreigners that it was not behind the dictatorial junta which Greek officers forced on their nation in April, 1967. And, though probably unjustified, rumors will persist that sinister forces organized the assassination of President Kennedy.

The idea of democracy no longer ignites the souls of men. When it does, as, for example, among certain militant groups of students, it means something quite different from what is meant by Presidents Johnson and Nixon. Often one asks oneself whether the term is being used honestly or merely for purposes of propaganda.

The shaky existence of the institution of democracy, once a dream of European reformers of the eighteenth and nineteenth centuries, becomes cruelly evident when we ask to what extent the democratization of the world, intended by the American government of World War I, has become a reality. At the beginning of World War II, only eleven European countries had authentic democratic institutions. Many Latin American countries had succumbed to totalitarian regimes. Even World War II did not essentially change the situation. True, Germany got rid of its dictator, but Russian communism gained immensely, and new totalitarian regimes emerged in Eastern Europe. Even if these satellite countries could establish some kind of democracy, as certainly many of their inhabitants desire, it certainly would not be the democracy of Wilson or Truman. The Hungarian and Czechoslovakian marchers for freedom were halted by Russian troops, while Yugoslavia and Romania are looking anxiously toward the mood of the Kremlin. The new African nations cannot, by their very nature, be democratic; in Eastern Asia, Communist China is the dominant power. Other nations, such as India and Indonesia, live in an extremely critical situation, balanced somehow by American money. Only the Scandinavian nations, the British Commonwealth, the Benelux countries, Switzerland, the United States, and Uruguay in Latin America have had a continuous democratic government during the twentieth century, with more and more of them changing the old idea of the personal responsibility of the citizen for his economic future into the policy of the welfare state.

The United States, so many critics fear, is becoming more and more a sort of computerized bureaucracy with at least as many, if not more, restrictions on the individual freedom of the citizen than the old monarchies. Most of the nations with a relatively long history of democratic institutions have lived under regimes that understood how to combine the monarchical tradition with the modern parliamentarian system. Instead of trying to restrict labor from political cooperation, as was the case in Germany and other Continental countries, their governments educated both the old privileged and the working classes toward political cooperation. In the United States, labor remained relatively unaffected by divisive ideological conflicts. It did not adopt the Marxian concept of *Klassenkampf,* nor did it form a third party. As a matter of fact, it partly achieved and still achieves its goal better by exercising pressure on the candidates of both the Republican and Democratic parties. Nevertheless, sporadic anarchist movements disquieted American society, especially in the 1880s and 1970s. In the 1880s, the International Workingman's Association numbered about eight thousand members who read such newspapers as the *Anarchist* in Boston and *Die Freiheit* (Liberty) in New York.

However, the absorbing power of the American economy, in combination with the severity of the prejudiced courts and the antianarchist laws of the legislation, succeeded in suppressing rebellious movements. On the whole, we seem to live in a period of waning ideologies. In the industrialized Western countries, the parties right and left of the middle, to a degree even Communist parties, converge toward the securing of common national interests, such as peace, prosperity, and equal chances for all. Everywhere, the cynic could say, the middle-class spirit has defeated its former adversaries. Everybody wants to remain or to become a bourgeois.

But what about the political spirit of the Soviet Russian? After surviving the bloody era of Stalin, the typical Russian has moved away from the resoluteness of his founding fathers; he is no longer akin to the early Bolshevik fighters. And this is natural, for no nation can live forever in a revolutionary mood. Only for the uprooted is revolution an end in itself. In spite of what we said about man's hatred against the tedious case of a mechanical and repetitive life, the adult, here and abroad, is anxious for order. He wishes to be steadily employed and to raise a family, to have some worthwhile purpose, and to have some leisure in order to remain healthy in body and spirit.

Thus, in the core of their desires, the Russians and the Americans are not far from each other. They are human beings who, first for all, want to survive.

With a democratic civilization in mind, should we speak of "prior" or "later"? Civilization is a whole. If we want not only to survive, but to live our own lives as self-respecting citizens, we should not think of ourselves primarily as members of an overorganized society constantly endangered by a new computerized bureaucracy, technocracy, and the military establishment. Rather, we should remember that it has always been the mark of a cultured nation that, despite the pressures of the immediate, it has felt a high regard for its prophets, thinkers, and artists. Their work is not a luxury to be enjoyed after the "really important things" are done but gives form to those deeper stirrings in the human soul without the cultivation of which even the important loses its finer qualities and sense of proportion. Culture is not only many discrete facts and demands; it is also the atmosphere we breathe, and despite all shortcomings, we breathe easier in democratic than in totalitarian countries. We do not throw those activists and writers who displease the powers at the top into jails or labor camps. Nevertheless, the "free" countries have also martyred fighters for freedom and perhaps are still doing so—mentally if not physically. And while engaged in competition with other social and ideological systems, we should remember that the Russians still live with the conviction that their fathers were the executors of the last great rebellion of the suppressed masses. Apparently, they and the nations on their side no longer believe in the Communist gospel as they did some decades ago. But that does not mean that they intend to adopt the American style of living. They find in it too much to criticize.

2. THE ECONOMY

I. The Inseparability of Economics and Politics

The continuous mingling of politics and economics is, as we have already seen, not entirely new. When in the Middle Ages, the feudal princes and the courts organized their wars, they engaged in huge financial enterprises, mostly with Jews as their advisers, who were experts in matters of money because they had long been permitted to lend it on interest. From the time of the first conquests of Portugal and Spain up to the nineteenth century, colonialism would have been impossible without the close relation between the state and the financial powers.

However, there was a difference. The transactions of earlier periods were not executed within a technostructure, the engineering of which requires the coordination of almost all forces available in a given society, not only those of strictly political, economic, and military, but also those of intellectual, moral, and scientific, nature.

One might venture the statement that since the French revolution declared the levée en masse in order to mobilize all available forces against the enemies, the modern nations have been in a continuous state of internal mutualism, with economic plus political power being the driving center.

There are good and evil sides in the increasing interaction between government and economy. The benefit lies in the fact that, as everywhere, concentration and cooperation are more efficient than division. The danger lies in the fact that we may no longer be able to escape the outreaching arms of the monster of finance and production. If, as in the case of Hitler, its machinery is conquered by ambitious leaders who understand how to force the might of the army and of the resources of wealth under their control, the result is the modern form of tyranny. According to John Kenneth Galbraith,[4] "in 1962 the five largest industrial corporations in the United States with combined assets in excess of $36 billion, possessed over 12 percent of all assets used in manufacturing assets. The 500 largest had well over two thirds. Corporations with assets in excess of $10,000,000, some 2000 in all, accounted for about 80 per cent of all the resources used in manufacturing of the United States. . . ."

It would nevertheless be wrong to assert that we live in a kind of tyranny of the big corporations. Although through lobbies, through their overt or covert contracts with politicians, and through their power over the means of communication, they exercise such an influence on the public mind and on our legislatures that many despair in the freedom and capacity of the latter to legislate for the benefit of the nation as a whole, there is certainly room left for political action on the part of the people. We are not yet "enslaved" by big business. Millions of employees, from the scientists to the workers, vote as free citizens and may even vote Socialist or Communist, as most of them do in Italy. Furthermore, beginning with the passage of the Interstate Commerce Commission Act of 1887 and the Sherman Antitrust Act of 1890, in the United States as well as in other countries, there is a large amount of regulatory legislation, extending from food control, licenses with regard to pharmaceutical products, the regulation of various markets and of the employment level over to the directing and redirecting of the national income to social purposes, such as health services, social security, housing, and education. Only the very rich could refuse today the benefits that accrue from various kinds of insurances provided by the originally much-combated welfare state. Far more than half of the expenses for scientific research is paid by the government; without such research, our industry would be outstripped by other countries, nor would our labor force be fully employed.

4. *The New Industrial State*, pp. 85-85, 16, 18.

Most governments now publish guidebooks based on surveys and inquiries possible only with the help of a large number of central agencies supported by a widespread network of diplomatic resources (including a goodly number of spies). Furthermore, only through the cooperation of statesmen with their economic advisers has it been possible to provide for large-scale international measures. All this justifies the statement of the famous British economist John Maynard Keynes that economists are "the trustees, not of civilization, but of the possibility of civilization." [5] During and after years of devastation caused by World War II, the foresight of American statesmen produced some of the greatest politico-economic measures in human history: first, the Lend-Lease Act of 1941, by which the United States supplied financial help to the anti-German countries on a basis to be determined after the war; then, the Marshall Plan (European Recovery Program), through which the United States allotted a sum of $17 billion to seventeen European nations, including Germany. The Marshall Plan saved Western Europe from total disintegration and from the certainty of Communist expansion.

Later, foreign-aid programs became a permanent feature of international economic and political relations. Point 4 of Truman's presidential address included assistance from the United States to underdeveloped nations. Today, all industrially advanced countries are engaged in some form of foreign aid, with all the implications which such aid involves with regard to the exchange of goods, international rivalry, and the expansion of influence in a world that, on the one hand, becomes smaller, and, on the other hand, increasingly complex.

Economists agree that the world situation demands intercontinental thinking, though in contrast to the 1930's, among the wealthier nations the problem is no longer one of encouraging shrinking production and investment but of finding suitable channels for the ever increasing output of commodities.

The various worldwide projects that individual nations have embarked on among themselves, or those which go under the

5. See Roy F. Harrod, *The Life of John Maynard Keynes* (New York: Harcourt, Brace, 1951), p. 194.

auspices of the United Nations, such as the Organization for Industrial Development (OID), the Research Institute for Social Development (UNRISD), a.o. as well as specialized agencies such as the Food and Agricultural Organization (FAO) and the various agencies for financial development or alliances among neighboring nations such as the European Economic Community (EEC) or Common Market, to mention but a few—all these can be considered only the beginning of an ever extending network of international economic cooperation.[6]

However, the obstacles to an economic world order are frightening. First, the national parliaments are, just like their constituencies, still too much under the influence of the traditional resistance against adequate grants for international purposes. They fail to recognize the danger to the future security and progress of their own country which may arise from the fact that over 50 percent of the world's population live in areas with such marginal food supplies that natural obstacles such as droughts, floods, and earthquakes can create massive famine.

Yet while most of the politically important nations (except Japan, which is forbidden to have an army) spend enormous sums on military preparedness,* they give only about one-thirtieth to one twenty-fifth of the total budget to international aid. Even if the amount were increased five times, as should be done in order to render the developing nations somewhat self-sustaining, we would still be far from an economically unified world. Rather, the highly industrialized and the poor countries tend to fall more and more apart.

Until the seventeenth century—before the Industrial Revolution in northern Europe—the working and living conditions among the various regions of the world were astonishingly similar. Afterward, the gap in the modes of production and output,

6. For a brief description of the various agencies see Jan Tinbergen, "International Economic Planning," in *Daedalus* (Spring, 1966).

* In the United States $80 billion a year—80 percent of the federal budget, 12 percent of the Gross National Product—is spent for military purposes. At the same time, about thirty-six million poor go hungry, the cities decay, and little if anything is done to combat the growing danger of pollution.

in the relation between individual work effort and production, and in the utilization of the soil and the treasures of the earth has widened rapidly. Without drastic economic measures, the gap will become too large to bridge, for with the best intentions the economically retarded nations will be incapable of raising per capita income and therefore domestic savings and internal investments. With the growing displacement by synthetics of raw materials, such as rubber, silk, and wood, the chances for profitable export will decrease unless domestic industries rise. For some time at least, they will be short of technically competent personnel. Additionally, the increase of population fostered by modern hygiene and by an aversion to birth control exactly on the part of those groups of the population which need it most support the opinion of experts who predict that the scales of the world's economic balance will not arrive at an equilibrium for fifty years. These experts, however, are called optimists by their more cautious colleagues who point to the findings of the International Food and Agriculture Organization that until 1980 forty million people may die of starvation if the present increase of the world population continues. Furthermore, they point to the fact that Western investors, who do well at home, have no incentives to take on the risks of investing and living in poor societies.

The disparity in the economic resources between the Northern and Southern Hemispheres is staggering. In the United States, the average annual income per capita is about $4,000; in the Federal Republic of Germany about $2,000; while in India and some African states it goes down to a few dollars and even less.

Actually, after the rise of an unknown and frustrated Austrian would-be artist Adolf Hitler who during World War I became a corporal in the German army, we should now have realized that nothing of any importance can happen at one place without, often in rapidly widening circles, affecting the whole world. Even fifteen years before Hitler, the Russian Lenin changed the aspect of the world by his combination of economic and political ideas. And let us remember, it was not so much the political totalitarianism of the new Russia which aroused the Western so-called freedom-loving countries as it was its *economic* totalitarianism. Otherwise they would not have allied themselves with the czarist system before and during World War I, though it was the very embodiment of medieval absolutism, which Germany was not. But the banks of republican France had invested millions of the money of its small depositors in Russia. The fear of losing this money in the case of a war between that country and threatening Germany induced France to accelerate a military showdown. In other words, there was a good deal of ideological hypocrisy in the slogan "to make the world safe for democracy." How, otherwise, could the United States and England, after the demise of the czar, have supported the White armies under reactionary generals who wanted to restore the czarist system? Not democratic ideals, but economic-pragmatic considerations, were behind the attitudes of the Western Allies to the Russian problem.

And would the United States really be so interested in preventing the expansion of communism in Vietnam and the adjacent countries if it were really a matter of democracy and not of safeguarding the commercial interests of a capitalist nation. Every knowledgeable person knew even before the American engagement in Vietnam that in developing countries democracy would be impossible, for it cannot be decreed by governments, least of all by foreign ones. It is the outcome of a long political and economic process, the development of which has taken the Western countries several hundred years and is not yet completed. Actually, democracy is more in jeopardy than ever, and though the Communist bloc is crumbling, it will not make room for democracy, as we would like to hope. Instead, confusion, chaos, and civil war may emerge.

II. Capitalism versus Communism

After fifty years of living side by side, capitalism and communism are no longer the same as they were. Whereas political chauvinism can drive men to actions which amount to self-destruction, the lessons they receive from economics are generally of a more sober and realistic nature, for there are at stake food and housing, buying and spending, production and employment. Perhaps only religious prejudice, when mixed with racial fanaticism, excels political hatred in insanity. Thus, the Spaniards impoverished their country by expelling the Moors and the Jews; the Hitlerites believed to have discovered the causes of all evil in a Jewish conspiracy; and in a less bloody, but nevertheless disastrous fashion, hungry India still feeds many thousands of sacred cows, to the despair of its enlightened statesmen.

Even the Soviet planners concede that extreme centralization has failed in one of the most important sources of living—in agriculture. Despite the vastness of their territories, they have had to rely on imports. Also, the industrial production of Soviet Russia—so surprisingly successful in its concentration on thermonuclear devices and space explorations—lags behind the original expectations of the needs of the country. Otherwise, the Russian government would not have invited Italian and French automobile companies to build large plants within Russian boundaries. Already before the conclusion of this deal in 1966, German, Austrian, and Swedish firms had cooperated with Hungarian, Polish, and Czech firms to build plants within Soviet territory and in India. The terms "coproduction" and "depolarization" have been added to the economic vocabulary.

On the other hand, as in politics so also in the economic realm, the capitalist countries have been forced more and more to modify the economic individualism of the bourgeois period. In the midst of democracy, originally based on the idea, "help yourself, otherwise you will perish," the welfare state emerged. The question arises, which we have already discussed in the previous chapter on politics with regard to the term "democracy"; to what degree do we carry with us polito-economic concepts from earlier decades of individualistic enterprise which are no longer correct in a situation? As has already been indicated, the state controls import and export and pumps billions into domestic welfare programs and foreign investments.[7]

The term "capitalist"—still unavoidable in large-scale historical and economic comparisons with the "precapitalist" societies of the past and the Communist societies of the present—no

7. A vivid description of the relation between government and private industry is to be found in an article by Emile Benoit, "Interdependence on a Small Planet," *Columbia Journal of World Business* (Spring, 1966).

longer carries with it the old Marxian contrast of the exploiting entrepreneur on the one side and the exploited proletarian on the other.

Surely, we live in a class society, and, to some degree, we will do so in the future. For wherever human beings gather, some move up, and others remain where they are—which usually means that they go downward. Some are talented and use their talents; others waste them. How rapidly and inevitably a society develops its elite, not only in a very few leaders, but institutionally—even though it claims to have abolished all inequality among men—becomes evident from the social development of Soviet Russia. It is governed by a relatively small political elite, represented by the Central Committee, which consists of 190 members. About 78.9 percent of them have had higher education, mainly in various fields of technology. Only 1.5 percent have no higher education. The education of the rest is unknown. Underneath these top men there stretches the larger level of the technocrat elite which amounts to 12 percent of the Soviet population. To this technocrat elite belong the educated specialists in the nonmanual labor force and the white-collar employees who in the party or in industry occupy somewhat responsible and decision-making positions—(though the latitude of decision-making is limited by the highly prescriptive character of the Communist system). The university training of both groups clearly separates them from the mass of the people. In 1967, the last year with available data of the already mentioned nonmanual labor force, 19 percent had complete or incomplete higher education, 47 percent had higher or specialized secondary education, and only 4 percent of the Soviet population of about 235,500,000 had complete or incomplete higher education. If one includes all those institutes which represent some kind of advanced training, including general secondary education, only 36 percent of the population have had some advanced training, complete or incomplete, beyond elementary education.[8]

8. The statistics are taken from Beatrice Beach, "The Education of Members of the Central Committee of the Communist Party of the Soviet Union," in *Comparative Education Review* (June, 1969), pp. 187ff. The statistics refer to the year 1967.

The Soviet citizen will rightly say that the elitism which characterizes the Soviet system in no way represents a class society as in the Western world in both earlier times and at present because of its hereditary system. No doubt, the heir of a great fortune is still a privileged man. Nevertheless, more and more observers of Russian society report that the children of the men in the higher ranks tend to remain within them, inasmuch as it is not only the title or the fortune a person inherits but the ambience he enjoyed in his childhood, such as the mental climate and the education in his family, the men and women with whom he is allowed to speak, and, last but not least, the social and profesional connections he is able to establish.

Thus, there is much likelihood that Soviet Russia, not to speak of other Communist countries, will also develop some kind of increasingly permanent class structure. Khrushchev's attempts at an educational reform were definitely motivated by this fear.

But, to return to our main topic, is an economic system still "capitalistic" in the older sense of the term where, as in the United States, about 26 million people hold stocks, or where, for example, in the German Volkswagen Company, the workers are co-owners of the enterprise? At several places—what a horrible idea for old businessmen—one seriously discusses the idea of comanagement between the workers and the directors of the plant. After all, in many corporations, the executive as well as the worker is an employe and may eventually be fired.

Only recently a French journalist called Germany the most revolutionary nation of the world in view of the high living standard of the workers. There, as well as in the Scandinavian countries, the term *"Klassenkampf"* has disappeared from the political vocabulary. In 1966, the German Social Democrats entered a coalition with the Christian Democrats, a middle-of-the-road group that grew out of the old Catholic Center party. In the United States the relation between management and labor is no longer as tense as it was some decades ago, though the ever increasing demands of the industrial unions (which already endanger the competitive power of this country) will create new tensions.

At the same time, the capitalistic animosity between industry and the welfare obligations of the state has given way to a degree of cooperation. Certainly, as everything in life, so also this new situation has its dangers, for it encourages the increase of the power of technocratic industrialism over the life of the people. Nevertheless, from a certain social point of view, it should be welcome. The big industries rightly feel that the problem of unemployment might be better solved if they take some of the burden away from the public bureaucratic agencies, which are overwhelmed by the magnitude of paperwork and which, in adition, invite corruption on both sides, among the givers as well as the receivers. Almost every large city in the United States has, or has had, a welfare scandal. It may be less expensive if, in a more decentralized system, industries create opportunities for occupational learning and through it new psychological incentives. For, as all the investigations in this field have shown, nothing is more detrimental to personal and collective morale than the lack of opportunity.[9]

Thus, in the widest sense of the term, might we not gradually change the term "capitalist democracy," originally connected with an economic system that since World War II has ceased to exist, into the more promising concept of "cooperative democracy." This cooperative society should extend its help to everyone who needs support, but it should not degenerate into a cradle for the lazy. Rather, it should make it clear to those who out of sheer indolence refuse to accept the offered opportunities for work that somehow they will be forced to earn their money for themselves. This may sound cruel, but still more cruel and self-destructive is a society that according to certain welfare reports sustains large families which for three generations have lived on welfare and at the same time complain that they do not have a good television set. Eventually they may even get one. The cruelty lies not only in the further corruption of already demoralized families but in their detrimental influence on their environment. For if, as the result of public housing programs, they are moved from old slums into new dwellings, they may soon make slums out of them.

9. See in this connection Chapter I in Robert Ulich, *Conditions of Civilized Living* (New York: Dutton, 1945).

During the depression, young people, hungry not only for food but also for a sense of purpose and useful employment, had to go into work camps. Why should not the willfully idle and therefore socially dangerous, despite their relatively small number, be placed into an environment where they have to do that amount of daily work which is necessary to pay for their maintenance? If this sounds like Hitler's or Stalin's concentration camps, the difference will be that in these camps they would have physical, occupational, and psychological counselors, intent on bringing them back to normal, communal, cooperative work.

In view of the temptation which for some people lies in guaranteed security without commensurate effort, one may doubt whether it is in the interest of the nation that the Nixon government, hightly disturbed by the bureaucratic inefficiency of the present welfare system, has planned a reform according to which every family could expect an annual minimum income. But even the Nixon reform could not avoid some control and bureaucratic difficulties.

Nevertheless, we and other nations in similar predicaments may learn from the comparison, and those eager to work may be less subject to humiliating supervision during the involuntary unemployment than before. On the other hand, those who do not miss the stimulation and self-respect that comes from productive activity may continue on the path toward idleness.

Man is a striving animal; otherwise he would not have survived. Take the spirit of effort and responsibility away from him, and he will degenerate. Sweden, admired for decades for its social legislation exceeds all other countries in the number of suicides and at least equals them in the rise of criminality, though no one there needs to feel the calamities of starvation or sicknes. We must aim toward a society that both demands and rewards individual effort and ambition provided they are restrained by the general willingness to harmonize individual success with the common weal. In other words, only within a system where the competitive drive in man and the community as a whole support rather than disrupt each other can we speak of a true democracy. But if the two colossuses of state and industry create a supersociety which collectivizes and thus desublimizes the soul of humanity (as Herbert Marcuse describes it in his *One-Dimensional Man*), we will have a human menagerie with most of the populace well kept but nevertheless poor. Aldous Huxley's *Brave New World* and George Orwell's *1984* would then become reality. There would be order but no happiness, busyness but no real life, and human beings but no humanity.

Therefore, exactly where the economic policies of capitalism and communism approach each other and even overlap, we should also be aware of the differences. We should do so exactly when we have the unity of mankind in mind, for without due respect for the personal and spiritual component in man, unity is merely another word fo coercive unification. Few things could be more horrible than a totalitarian world government.

Therefore, just as in his dealings with the state the democratic citizen must stubbornly defend his civil rights, so also as a member of the economic order he must not jeopardize his privilege to choose his vocation in accordance with his talent and resources to own, acquire, and administer property beyond the mere necessities of living; to assume the risk of management of his business, however small; in short, to act as a participant and not merely as a wheel in the economic apparatus. Certainly, even here the lines are blurred. Is a worker or even the wealthy executive in Detroit not also a wheel in a gigantic machine driven by the inhuman force of capitalist technology and competition? And where, on the other side of the scale, is the economic freedom of the slum dweller?

Ultimately, however, freedom, though not separable from material goods, is a human quality which transcends both the political and the economic realms. One can be rich and live in ambience with innumerable chances for action, yet be unfree. The rich playboy is the least free man on earth, for freedom is always connected with a lasting goal to which the person can devote himself. Only through constructive devotion can a mass of mortals be formed into a community of authentic human beings.

III. Specific Features of the Postwar Era

Our technological society offers innumerable advantages: health, longevity, comfort, mobility, and education. For this we should be grateful. A goodly number of the most vociferous critics of our "mechanized and soulless mass culture" would not be alive without the mechanism of surgery. Why, then, such a widespread feeling of uneasiness? Is it merely because people who have more demand ever more? Or are there deeper reasons?

Certainly, one of the reasons for the uneasiness is the fact that *our present civilization is the most artificial product* the human mind has ever created—magnificent in a way, but a threat to the inextricable desire of man not to be totally divorced from nature. Man wants to be an entity of his own, growing according to his immanent trends toward self-realization instead of being the product of an environment so complex that he stands before it as before a gigantic machine, the working of which he cannot understand. We miss in our life the flavor of naturalness, just as we miss it in an artificial flower. Such a flower may be more gaudy than a clover blossom or a rose. The rose may even be perfumed, but it is never the wonder of a real rose. Or take a chest made by an artisan and a modern factory product. The former is harmonious and at the same time delightfully uneven; the latter is just accurate. But we put artificial flowers on our chests, both bought from a department store, because for a natural flower and a hand-made piece of furniture we otherwise so rich people have no money.

There is another reason that prevents us from fully enjoying the advantages of our civilization. This is *the vulnerability of our complex modern life.* When thinking of vulnerability, we immediately remember the atomic bomb. But even without this murderous instrument we would feel the exposure. The simplest household of today depends on hundreds of media which in turn depend on hundreds of other media. The self-sustaining family that in some parts of the Western world sporadically existed even until the end of the nineteenth century is now a myth, or an anthropological phenomenon of rapidly disappearing primitive cultures. Hence, the concept of freedom becomes more and more illusory. Instead of the concreteness of action it had at the time of Thomas Jefferson, it has become a psychological concept; it has retreated into the inner precincts of the soul. But thinking without the chance of acting becomes in the course of time a professional affair.

A third element of unrest in modern culture is its *obsession with speed,* mainly as a competitive device. But, as such, it is self-defeating. If everyone uses a jet, no one arrives earlier than the other. Nevertheless, a businessman or a reporter might miss a plane in New York and be some in Calcutta hours later than his competitor.

Our schools have courses in speed reading, or "power reading," but they have no courses in slow and careful reading. Assignment for the next week: read, and report about three books —each of which may have caused the author several years to write. The Sheraton Hotels advertise their capacity "To unwind the keyed-up executive," depicted with a briefcase in his left hand and a key stuck in his back. What will help him unwind? Perhaps a few martinis before dinner.

Speed creates noise and pollution of the air. Therefore, the dream of the young businessman is to be able to escape to a farm, or even to a yacht, just as the boss does. Thus, the dream of recreation at the bosom of nature becomes at the same time the much coveted symbol of success—new stimulus in an already overstimulated environment. But how many can even think of such luxuries? They may have vacation, but despite a relatively good income they cannot pay for a few weeks at the seashore or in the mountains. The resorts are too expensive for a family with children; therefore, the trailer. Camp counselors tell us that it takes youth from the crowded areas of New York or Chicago about three weeks to lose their fear of silence. They cannot live in surroundings without radio, television and the rattle of buses. But when they are adjusted and begin to breathe the quiet of the air, they must go home.

Thus we encounter a paradox. On the one hand, modern man is wealthier, stronger, taller, more athletic, and longer lived than his ancestors. On the other hand, he is nervous and sleepless; he cannot meditate or pray. Even those who should have much reason for contentment cannot find it. And just as internationally the rich and the poor countries become more and more divided from each other, so also within the same nation the gulf widens between those who have too much and those who have too little. The American Senate Hunger Committee has brought out expert testimony that twenty million Americans are living in poverty and that over one-third of the children of the poor are so anemic that they should be placed in hospitals before going to school.

Our analysis of the postwar economy would be incomplete if we did not add a short description of some specific changes within the *internal structure of business itself.*

(1) *The Individual Entrepreneur versus the Corporation.* No longer, as in the bourgeois era, is industrial society dominated by hundreds of relatively small entrepreneurs who reigned as the economic, often also as the political, bosses in their communities. There they might either have been revered as the benefactors who paid for the care of the old elm trees along the shadowy and dignified streets of the town, who supported the nascent public library, who helped to erect the first hospital and brought new life and prosperity into the sleeping community. They lived in mansions that were the awe of the townspeople, collected treasures on their journeys around the world, and received honored guests with whom they discussed the merits and demerits of slavery and the American Constitution. But there were others who brought new methods of cheap mass production, hired badly paid foreign workers, and ruined the business of the old artisans and small landowners. For their dwellings they built pompous atrocities with innumerable gables, chimneys, and colored windows, paid for, as the rising number of Socialist agitators preached in the tavern, with "the sweat of the exploited proletarian worker."

Today the old entrepreneur has been replaced by enormous corporations which fabricate the bulk of the nation's products. They operate with capital investments which, except for a few cases, as may survive in some mining, oil, and real estate speculations, by far exceed the capital even of the wealthiest man on our planet. We have already discussed them.

(2) *Planning and Group Decision.* It is evident that in a political-economic situation such as ours, long-range planning and forecasting is one of the principal means of political and economic success.

There was, of course, some general planning also in the bourgeois period (without some degree of planning mankind would not have survived), but this planning occurred in the heads of the entrepreneur and his few friends, while today it is the result of deliberation of financial and technical experts, of production specialists, market researchers, bankers, and of government officials. Without such cooperation, the crisis of the French franc in November, 1968, would have brought about an international catastrophe. Nevertheless, it is a myth to believe that even in a large corporation individual initiative, imagination, and the courage of responsibility become unnecessary.[10] The only difference is that these qualities are now cooperatively controlled by boards of advisers, trustees, shareholders, and an increasingly complex number of political circumstances. Furthermore, the head of a modern corporation and his assistants are highly educated. By far the large majority of them have advanced college degrees in such fields as law, economics, or engineering. The time of the self-made man with but a minimum of formal education is gone, and so is the time of the old forms of learning merely by practical apprenticeship. Nor has the grand-scale adventurer any place in our computerized business world.

(3) *Advertising and Communication.* When looking at a newspaper or weekly as it appeared at the end of the nineteenth century, one finds little advertising. In a small community the grocer announced the arrival of a box of herring or a set of tools, or a traveling circus sent word of coming. All this amounted only to a small part of a publisher's income. It was somewhat different in the larger countries, especially in the

10. For a short and excellent analysis of management as an "art" see Eli Goldston, "Universities and the Market Place," *Bulletin,* The American Academy of Arts and Sciences, Vol. XXIII.

United States, where new methods of influencing the public mind were more quickly discovered. The circus owner Phineas T. Barnum, "the father of modern publicity," and his associate, James A. Bailey, used all possible fanfare to excite the expectations of people. Soon, theaters, cosmetics firms, and political parties used the kiosk, the walls of buildings, and the press to capture the interests of potential customers.

Today there exists a reciprocal relation between the businessman and the press, including radio and television. Neither one could live without the other. The departments of public relations and advertising are among the most important to a corporation; they have to translate the work of the firm into attractive language. The new automobile and washing machine or the new drugs and soap are infinitely superior to any other product. And which woman would not attract the eyes of men if dressed according to the fashions offered by the department store on main street? Results: if a public school teacher wears the same dress for several days the pupils ask her whether she sleeps in it. The purpose is achieved. Even children are pressured into expectations far beyond the necessary.

On the other side, the agent of the advertising company has to lobby at innumerable anterooms of business executives and their assistants in order to show them that they would invite bankruptcy without his cooperation (as some did during the Great Depression). Thus, the serious reader who wants to be informed about the essentials of our political and cultural life has to turn over dozens of pages in order to find—mostly on the inner and least recognizable side of the page—the continuation of an article on international politics or religious issues. A visitor from a Communist country, however much he may envy the freedom of our press, certainly does not covet an American who wants to read a profile or a short story in the *New Yorker*.

All this indicates much more than can be seen at the first glance. It is an example of the most polar phenomenon in our modern life; on the one hand, the rapid accessibility of every event, at home and abroad, important or unimportant; on the other hand, the captivity of so many of our contemporaries in a network of influences which cause him to lose more and more

his sense of individuality and of proportion. His taste, his desires, and, to a degree, his whole value system are determined
by the daily impact of advertising on his mind. More and more
demands are created, and more and more "necessities" of living
are recommended, the acquisition of which may cause more un-
happiness than contentment. The rich are emulated instead of
the excellent; mere newness is mistaken for originality; and one
of the most sinister capacities of man, envy, is constantly
aroused. So often one can read the story of a humble policeman
or a bank clerk who came in conflict with law and had to go
into prison because his wife upset his carefully worked-out
installment plan by purchasing the same expensive television
set as the wife of the neighbor who earned enough.

No one can accurately measure the influence of advertising
in our means of communication. No doubt, good newspapers
cannot be bought with money; nevertheless, they can pay their
often excellent journalists and columnists only through the profit
they derive from their advertisers. To alienate them might invite disaster. The relation between advertising agencies and the
radio and television industry is a disgrace to this country. Our
better information media will not tell us total untruth (which,
after all, is too easily discovered), but we may not hear the total
truth either if the news comes from the Pentagon and other
partial sources. Visitors from foreign countries are often surprised at the ignorance of educated Americans about the reasons
why so many walls in foreign cities contain the slogan "Yankee
go home."

(4) *The "New Estate" and the Education of the Businessman.*
Nowhere is the change from the old entrepreneur society into
the new technocratic, planning, and managerial society more
clearly reflected than in the rise of what we may call a "new
estate." Here also the old sociological vocabulary has become
obsolete. In earlier times, one divided the body politic into
three estates: the nobility; the clergy; and the third estate, the
members of the latter sometimes called by contemptuous noblemen *les roturières* or *les canailles.* With any one of them a nobleman did not duel, however great the offense may have been

afflicted upon him, for only noble blood was worth the risk of fighting for the sake of honor.

The situation became confused in the nineteenth century. In Germany, officers as well as students of fighting corporations, whether of noble or common origin, engaged in duelling. In France, all men of honor were allowed to participate in this nonsense. In certain countries of South America political enemies still cross swords.

With the rise of the industrial system, there appeared the fourth estate, often called the proletariat, a term which, as has already been said, has almost disappeared in the more advanced countries. Yet, it is sometimes difficult to avoid another uncomplimentary term—"the masses"—for that amorphous though in itself highly differentiated stratum of our industrial society, which is composed mainly of the blue-collar workers and their families.

However, let us not forget two facts. First, today, many blue-collar workers earn more than struggling individuals with college degrees. Second, if the term "masses" connotes lack of individuality, many wage earners may belong less in that category than millions of well-dressed citizens of all professional levels. Often it seems that the surest way to deprive a person of originality is to expose him to a protracted education. Whereas the old hierarchy of estates has lost much of its meaning, we might still use the term "estate" to signify the appearance of a new and special social group. Every generic label for this group would be wrong. But as we so loosely use the term "bureaucrat," we may dare use here the term "technical expert." Its representatives are related to the scholar by their often extensive academic training; but, in contrast to the old-fashioned university professor, they use their knowledge in a definitely utilitarian fashion, as advisers to brokerage firms or banks, in the laboratories of industrial plants, in government agencies, in the communications systems, and sometimes in highly refined technological enterprises they have started themselves. In every one of these places they have a much higher income than they would have in a university, for, in addition to the official salary, they may increase their fortune through intimate knowledge of business transactions and priority options on stocks. They are the "problem-solvers," whose moral conscience is sometimes less developed than their intelligence. They may serve as missile specialists for one year to one country and, a few years later, serve in the same capacity to one hostile to the former—and even receive honorary degrees for their services. These men are the *condottiere* of modern technocracy.

Fortunately, such mercenary soldiers in the competitive war between modern industries and nations are still rare. Pejorative epithets apply only to a few of our modern experts; the large majority are dedicated men, disciplined not only intellectually but also ethically, because they transfer the accuracy, required by their training and their work, to their personal style of living.

But it is not only the problem-solver, or technical expert, who forms a special group or a kind of estate in our modern society such as did not exist in the era of the bourgeois. Even then, an increasing number of higher schools of technology trained the academic engineer or chemist. Nevertheless, his appointment, his status, and his function were different from those of the modern expert, who resembles more a free lancer with somewhat permanent affiliations than the old-fashioned technical designer who generally worked in close contact with both the owner of his company and the foreman and the plant. Something similar applied also to the old type of chemist in pharmaceutical firms, though he was perhaps more separated from the workers in the plant.

Fundamental changes have also appeared in the preparation and the role of the leaders of the modern business world. Before and during the bourgeois era, a businessman was educated in the firm of his father and his father's friends. About a hundred years ago the first higher schools of business appeared. They were looked on with suspicion by the older generation of merchants just as much as they were by the universities, which disdained the "utilitarian" character of the newcomer. Today Harvard's School of Business Administration is one of the nationally and internationally most famous departments of Harvard

University. Executives, already advanced in their careers, go there to learn about the management and psychology of large-scale enterprises. These highly trained leaders in the modern world of management, constantly cooperating with their technological advisers or perhaps growing out of their ranks, determine to a large degree the course of modern history and will do so ever more as a result of their close interconnection with politicians. Whereas in earlier times politics was considered the *nobile officium* of a prominent citizen, chosen for his merits in the community, today the chief requirement for election to public office is wealth or access to the finances available for radio and television time, for advertising and press coverage, in some countries, even for large-scale bribing reaching down into dark corners of the underworld. It is this power of money which gives the leaders of our industrial and financial enterprises a monopoly in the field of politics.

It would be unrealistic to deny the importance of the profit motive for the man of business and therefore his preference for a candidate and a party nearest his own interests. The question is whether, blinded by the lure of immediate gain, he follows the next, though perhaps sordid, road toward success, or whether he places his thoughts and actions in a wider frame of responsibility.

The picture is not encouraging. About 1930, German industrialists lent money to Hitler to build up his party, which had already begun to decline; and in the United States many industrialists, though not all, supported one of the most insane and inane adventures in human history—the Vietnam war. Perhaps the phrase "military-industrial complex," is sometimes used too loosely. Nevertheless, as John Kenneth Galbraith shows in his book *How to Control the Military*,[11] during the fiscal year of 1968, 57 percent of the nation's defense contracts ($24 billion worth) were awarded without competitive bidding, and nearly seven hundred generals, admirals, and navy captains were employed by the ten largest defense contractors. Even if one takes into account the fact that these men can give expert advice

11. New York: Doubleday, 1969.

to the producers of modern weapons, the number suggests subtle forms of bribery which may not be punishable by law but which are nevertheless unethical. And the briber is not less guilty than the bribed. There have been many cases of price fixing, of intentionally sloppy design, and General Motors set spies on the path of Ralph Nader, a man who revealed the existing hazards of certain types of automobiles. Despite all the progress in modern industrial design and all the endeavors to save the beauty of the American landscape and the purity of our air and waters, the inroads of reckless industrial enterprise into the life of the citizen increase from year to year.

It sounds, therefore, utopian that one of the outstanding French scholars and businessmen, Joseph Basile, in his book *La Formation intellectuelle des cadres et des dirigeants*,[12] demands an industrial and financial elite, or an aristocracy of enterprise, which—freed from the burden of cumbersome calculation by automation, computers and other brain-saving devices—will restore the lost balance of our world by virtue of their technical knowledge, the universality of their interests, their capacity of understanding and handling their fellow men, their sense of beauty, their creativeness, and their courage of responsibility; briefly, through their whole style of living.

To repeat, this sounds utopian. But as of all utopias, also this one is partially right. Its truth consists of the affirmation that if today the statesmen in the field of economy and industry, just as much as their political companions, continue to be merely profit-making technocrats or power-seeking politicians without a profound sense of social responsibility, our culture may increasingly turn into a human anthill, with everybody being busy losing his humanity.

But here we turn from the field of economics to the fields of religion, humanism, and education, which will constitute the last segment of the book.

12. Verviers: Gerard, 1967.

Chapter 6

RELIGION, HUMANISM, AND EDUCATION

*Neither do men put new wine into old bottles:
else the bottles break, and the wine runneth
out, and the bottles perish; but they put new
wine into new bottles and both are preserved.*
Matt. 9:17

1. RELIGION

When later generations go through the records of our time—
books, journals, conference reports, public addresses, and private
letters—they may well agree that the greatest bewilderment in
our era of general disarrangement reigned in the field of religion.

They will read that Christianity was crumbling before the
onslaught of science and technology; that people did not believe
in God, least of all some professors of theology; that morality
and law had lost their moorings in the greater order and were,
therefore, on such a low ebb. They will read that everywhere
church attendance and religious interest declined during the
1960's. In 1969 the United States had about 321,000 churches
with an avowed membership of about 126 million members; but
only 50 percent, probably less, attended church with some fre-
quency; the rest were indifferent. Religious seminaries were
searching for qualified students. Catholic priests got married,
and in 1969 about 6,000 of the 167,000 Roman Catholic nuns
renounced their vows, while an increasing number of Protestant
clergymen left their denominations.

On the other hand, they will hear that divided Christendom
made a step toward inner unity; that the old conflict between
faith and empiricism was disappearing because of a new inter-

pretation of the Christian Gospel; and that—at least in the United States—the number of churchgoers increased. This country, so they will be told, never had such a rich religious life. The various denominations built new churches; sold an enormous quantity of attractively bound Bibles; organized dances and innumerable activities for young and old; and invested billions in breweries, publishing houses, banks, and real estate.

As far as possible, let us attempt to find some path through the thicket of contradiction. When in the grip of danger and anxiety—as all men are in the atomic age—they are sharply reminded of the threat that hangs over all life. And in order to gain a measure of inner assurance, many of them turn to something which to them is sacred, or absolute and unconditional, even though they may not pray to a personal God or pray at all. They have lost their trust in man, for they have seen human masses behaving worse than beasts. Thus, after the lull in religious interest which characterized the eighteenth and nineteenth centuries, people all over the world discuss religion. Even the young Communists, though convinced of the antiquatedness of Christianity, ask for books about religion. At the same time that men set foot on distant planets, they feel their littleness in the ever widening expanses of the universe. What is life? Where does the human being belong? Does his history have a deeper meaning, or will some time the curtain fall and the play be over? The more we learn, the more lonely we become.

After the horrors of Hitler, many Jews would have felt like deserters if, as in happier decades, they had forgotten their past and no longer remembered the solemn rituals which adorn the milestones of their long history. Also, bewildered Christians seek to discover a new meaning in symbols and ceremonies which have become meaningless. Whereas national songs and myths divide, just as religious institutions did in earlier times and still do to a degree, men of goodwill, partly encouraged by the ecumenical movement, hope that the discovery of the common human depth element in all religions may help them in their endeavor toward the spiritual and the political unity of mankind.

Critical Christians, however, wonder whether it adds to the prestige of the papacy if it so frequently sends pious exhortations into the deaf ears of rivaling powers, especially since in the past the clergy of all denominations has consistently sided with the forces of reaction and blessed troops in unjust wars, such as the Vietnam conflict. This war, so these critical Christians suspect, would not have arisen without the understandable resentment of Buddhists and their priests against the growing influence of a but recently converted Christian minority that has profited from its betrayal of the older tradition, both politically and economically. And the rumors persist that it was partly on the insistence of the Vatican that President Eisenhower sent so-called advisers to Vietnam.

The churches, especially the Catholic church, have always been masters in the subtle art of politics, overt and especially covert. Only recently a growing number of Catholic and Protestant ministers have openly entered the field of direct social action and have dared to support the anti-Vietnam war marchers, striking laborers, protesting blacks, and desperate slum dwellers.

In the United States the churches have increased their membership, though most of them, including the Catholic church and the major Protestant denominations, not in relation to the increase of the population. During the year 1969 the Catholic church reported a membership gain of less than one percent, the smallest in twenty-five years, while the Lutheran bodies gained only two-tenths of one percent. A visitor of the services of these churches will find a large majority of women and older people, and this applies to all Western countries.

It proves the general craving for symbolism and spiritual stability in a time of change—a form of escapism, as the rationalist would say—that the dogmatic and authoritative churches have enjoyed a robust growth. The Mormon church has continuously established new congregations all over the world, and so has the Assemblies of God, America's largest pentecostal body. In contrast, the liberal churches, though actually more in harmony with modern knowledge, are in a critical situation.

Viewing the whole picture, one cannot deny that interest in religious problems has increased. This, however, does not contradict the fact, deplored most of all by the clergy itself, that typical church membership among the more enlightened middle classes has more than ever become a matter of sociality and convention. In smaller communities of the United States, going to church seems to secure confidence and social prestige, and it may be wiser for a young businessman, lawyer, physician, or teacher to conform than to express "leftist" opinions about God and the world. To small minds, religious conservatism seems to be a symbol of political reliability and moral trustworthiness. Therefore, shrewd politicians shake hands with the preacher, evoke the blessing of God in their endeavors, however evil, and kiss babies. Abraham Lincoln refused to do this.

The French writer Charles Maurras said once that the French are unbelievers; but, as a matter of course, they all are good Catholics. They want their children baptized, their marriages blessed, and their dead properly buried. During the past decades, political parties put the word "Christian" before their trade name, advertising thereby their claim to stay and act within the Christian heritage.

Up to some years ago, a teacher in the public schools of Tennessee and Arkansas acted illegally when teaching the "heresy" of evolution, and in 1966 the Iowa supreme court ruled against a father who wanted his young son to return to him and his second wife's custody on the grounds that he "is either an agnostic or atheist and has no concern for formal religious teaching." He is also "a political liberal." It did not improve the father's chances that he had moved away from the "safe" pastures of Iowa to sinful California.[1]

The churches influence politics, social life, and education far beyond the actual membership of churchgoers, which in the countries of Western Europe number not more than 8 to 20 percent of the mature population, mainly women and old people. Even in the most Catholic part of Germany, Bavaria, at least two-thirds of all churchgoers are women; there they also vote for the more conservative parties. However, the more advanced their education, the more independent they become.

1. *New York Times*, February 26, 1966.

Through their missionary activities and charitable and educational institutions, the Christian churches penetrate even large parts of the Far East. But there is little prospect that they will turn any considerable parts of the Asian populations away from their religious roots. Often missionaries have caused a dangerous split in the inner life of the so-called pagans.[2] Instead of finding a new spiritual mooring, they have been uprooted.

On the other side of the spiritual landscape, liberal and critical minorities suffer from lack of organization. Individualistically minded, as their members are, they elude a convenient label. There is no generic name for them. In some American circles, especially among political investigators, the name "liberal" is almost as bad as "Communist." It does not count that these liberals may take religious, moral, and political problems more seriously than their opponents. This is perhaps the very reason why they are suspect.

Of course, in the realm of the mind as well as in the political realm, the number of the truly involved has always been small. Not to care is always more comfortable than to care. Most people are too busy with other things: their professional advancement, their family, their taxes, and perhaps their clubs. Even in our era of affluence, the energy of many is absorbed by the daily battle of survival, a battle that becomes all the more serious the more the goods of comfort and luxury entice the buyer.

But there is a deeper reason for indifference than lethargy. It cannot be denied that the most basic tenets of Christianity are strangers to our contemporary intellectual conscience. Christianity, wrote Alfred North Whitehead in his *Religion in the Making*,[3] has been incapable of an adequate metaphysical system because it has "no clear-cut separation from the crude fancies of older tribal religions." Indeed, the Christian religion has been the scene of as many doubts, sometimes bordering on cynicism, as of heroic acts of faith. Many saints were tortured by qualms of unbelief, while systematic theologians spoke of the *absurdum* in the Christian dogma and postulated a special "divine grace" for assisting the weak mortal in his battle for faith

2. *Der Spiegel*, September 1, 1969, p. 34.
3. Cleveland and New York: World, Meridian Books, no year, p. 200.

and salvation. Even a questioning child feels his scruples about the veracity of biblical stories, while the thinking adult will wonder why so many dangerous superstitions and taboos, tolerated or at least advocated by the great religious systems of the world, still prevent the full utilization of modern knowledge for the benefit of mankind. For example, within the Catholic church one such taboo is the opposition to birth control and to abortion when the mother is in danger.

Nevertheless, as has already been said in earlier chapters, exactly the poetical and decorative elements, in Christianity as well as in other faiths, have lifted millions above the dreary uniformity of their daily life and inspired artists and dreamers, thinkers and prophets. Even the occult, such as astrology, is to some minds more fascinating than demonstrable truth. Logic and analysis are strenuous, while the continual assertion of atheism is boring, as everything is that begins with a negative prefix. Even those religions which started on a high and somewhat abstract intellectual level, such as Hinduism and Buddhism, had to tolerate the accretion of the fairy tale and the fantastic in order to satisfy the mystical instinct in man. Yet, the miraculous alone cannot sufficiently nourish the human soul. If a creed demands a belief that cannot be honestly believed, it invites inner tension, or becomes a pious fraud.

Inevitably, theologians who wish to reconcile the teaching of Christ and the Apostles with modern thought find themselves in a precarious situation. Perhaps only in politics reigns as much gibberish and self-contradiction as is formed in our theological discussions. Historically, of course, the dilemma between faith and intellect is not new. As early as six hundred years ago medieval Schoolmen argued about the compatibility between divinely revealed truth, or the *ratio divina*, on the one hand, and, on the other hand, truth according to human intelligence, or the *ratio humana*. The lack of agreement about the two verities caused the decline of Christian Scholasticism at the end of the Middle Ages. Henceforth, the gap has been immensely widened by the whole progress of thought and science since the Renaissance.

I. The Protestant Situation

Thus, by a thorough process of "demythologization" and by the change of concepts, previously supposed to be based on facts, into mere symbols devoid of clear reference, the *avant-garde* of modern theologians—among them Rudolf Bultmann, Paul Tillich, and Dietrich Bonhoeffer—tries to separate the time-conditioned and superstitious elements in Christianity from its eternal essence.

They have abandoned the old dualism between matter and mind in favor of a monistic world view. Such central doctrines as the Holy Trinity, original sin, the cross, and immortality are given existentialist meanings which in earlier times would have been condemned into the abyss of heresy. No layman could have expressed the doubts of a contemporary skeptic more courageously than did John Robinson, suffragan bishop of Woolwich and author of *Honest to God*, in a broadcast under the auspices of the British Broadcasting Corporation. "With this in mind I would ask to expose yourself to the three thrusts of modern atheism. . . . They may be represented in three summary statements. God is intellectually superfluous; God is emotionally dispensable; and God is morally intolerable." [4]

In the United States the late Episcopal Bishop James A. Pike of San Francisco could remain in his office until September, 1966, though in the course of time he had given up one after the other of the fundamental tenets of Christianity, except the idea of immortality. (He believed he had conversed with his deceased son.) After many deliberations, the bishops of his denomination did not dare convene a heresy trial, certainly for fear that the ensuing discussion might have revealed an embarrassing uncertainty among the judges themselves.

The typical clergyman in an educated Protestant congregation finds himself in an ambiguous situation. He has lost his mooring in a firm conviction which safeguards a man against being drowned in the waves of doubt. He wishes to appear mod-

4. Quoted from *The Listener and BBC Television Review,* January 13, 1966, p. 55.

ern and open-minded; yet he is embarrassed when an impolite questioner asks for his opinion about the Crucifixion, the Resurrection, and the Eucharist. He feels safer talking about the moral and educational value of religion than about matters of creed.

Politically, he may perhaps incline more toward the left then the right, but he is afraid of alienating his congregation through openly taking sides. Thus, he prefers to take refuge to the utterances of the leaders of his church (who today are sometimes more broad-minded than some parishioners would like them to be). Or he discusses controversial books in a disengaged and semiobjective way. Concerning sex, he wavers between tolerance and tradition, just like the parents who would like to have his advice. He can remain in a state of happy balance only when he does not search too radically into his own self. A growing number of those who are supposed to be the guides of the soul go to a psychoanalyst. But how can a thinking person take comfort when he reads such gibberish as suppressed by the leaders of American Protestantism about the mission of the church:

> The Church's mission in the midst of this social revolution is both theological and practical. . . .
>
> Theological, in the primary sense in which the Church's calling is always theological: we are a peculiar people on whom God has laid the obligation to seek to discern his initiative in the particular events of time and place. . . .[5]

The future will decide whether the new group of Protestant theologians will bring about the self-renewal of Protestantism or whether they represent the rear guard in a losing battle between Christianity and modernity. Certainly, they have tried to inject new modes of meaning into the old Christian vocabulary, but they have done so at the costly price of an ambiguity that, to put it mildly, evades the generally accepted rules of verification

5. *Christian Outlook*. Massachusetts Council of Churches, Boston (October, 1969).

and logical consistency.[6] One should not claim to be within a religious tradition if one interprets it by dint of self-invented concepts which are entirely different from its original intention and if one oscillates so that one's views are compatible with any standpoint whatsoever—orthodox, liberal, or agnostic.

Such twilight appeals to those minds which are afraid of clear decisions. They can indulge in the modern "anguish" and "anxiety" of "existential loneliness" and the "despair of self-alienation." At the same time, convinced of the "paradoxical-ness" and inner "dialectic" of all religious experience and of life as a whole, they can still persuade themselves that their un-belief is but another form of Christian involvement. They can still feel anchored in the "ground of being," irrespective of whether there dwells in it a personal God, or a God beyond the God, or no God at all.

Inevitably, there appeared a new group of Protestant think-ers, called the "godless theologians," represented by such men as Gabriel Vahanian, William Hamilton, Paul Van Buren, Thomas Altitzer, and Harvey Fox.[7]

The "death-of-God" theologians do not express identical opin-ions. Indeed, few labels are so misleading as the one under which they have to march, though they themselves are partly responsi-ble for the general uncertainty. Thomas Altitzer and William Hamilton, in the Preface of their book, *Radical Theology and the Death of God*,[8] offer ten possible definitions of the various meanings of the phrase "God is dead." These definitions move from radical atheism and the religious indifference of modern man to mystical visions of God's death on the cross. All the death-of-God theologians are motivated by the hope that a thorough overhauling of Christianity and a new moral inter-pretation of Christ's teaching will save the ship from sinking.

If we look for influences, we can easily detect Kierkegaard; Nietzsche; Karl Barth's supranaturalist interpretation of God as

6. See Paul Edwards, "Professor Tillich's Confusions," *Mind*, Vol. LXXIV (1965), pp. 192-214.

7. The theological ideas of these writers are explained by Charles N. Bent, S.J., *The Death-of-God-Movement* (New York: Paulist Press, 1967).

8. New York: Bobbs-Merrill, 1966.

the "Wholly Other"; as well as Tillich's criticism of supranaturalism; Bultmann's demythologization; existentialist writers such as Camus, Kafka, and Sartre; and, finally, modern semantics. But in spite of the semantic influence, the godless theologians fail to make it sufficiently clear whether they speak of God as a reality or as a subjective human conception. It is the same lack of clarity that already appears in early Christian mysticism and finally leads to the arrogant verse in Rilke's *Stundenbuch* (Book of Hours) "*Wo wärst du, Gott, wenn ich nicht wäre*" (Where, God, would you be if I were not). Man, then, is the creator of God, instead of God being the creator of man. But whatever their differences, all the death-of-God theologians agree that we live in an era of the gradual dilution of the ideas which pious men of earlier times connected with the idea of God. They also agree that this process is just as much due to the abrasive influence of modern theology itself as to modern secularism.

The critical reader will understand the concern of a modern Protestant theologian about the future of his faith and of the unperceptive and often vulgar use of the name of God.* Yet, in spite of the medley of confused and confusing concepts, he seems to be incapable of including in his reflections the deeply religious potentialities of modern science, enlightenment, and humanism.[9]

Despite considerable publicity, the dialogue between the clergymen and the nonexisting God has so far remained within a relatively small circle. A chasm yawns between advanced Protestant religious philosophy and typical denominational teaching and preaching. But the crisis appears there, too. What was once the pride and center of Protestant worship, the sermon, becomes an increasingly difficult undertaking, while the religious literature for the young and for the Sunday schools spans the

---

* I once found at the door of a Protestant church the following announcement of a sermon: "God rolls his sleeves up."

9. The journal which attempts to bring about a synthesis between religion and science is *Zygon, Journal of Religion and Science,* published since 1966 under the editorship of Ralph Wendell Burhoe. See also Robert Ulich, *A History of Religious Education* (New York: New York University Press, 1968).

whole gamut from the old ponderous and incomprehensible catechism to pious trivialities with pictures of Jesus as a nice fellow in the bourgeois environment of suburbia, totally incapable of ever making an enemy. The problem emerges, first raised by Rousseau, and then taken up about 1800 by the great liberal theologian Friedrich Schleiermacher: can and should religion be taught to the immature?

If history is right in telling us that the ideas of a few eventually became the ideas of many, then Protestantism will go through the severest crisis it ever had. At the end of the crisis, it will either look like a broken mosaic, or the present revolution will prove its right to the title of the *ecclesia semper reformanda.* But if one listens to certain modern theologians, the new *ecclesia* will resemble more a union of religious agnostics than an old sacredotal institution of pious believers.

II. The Catholic Situation

Against the background of growing secularism, what will be the future of the Catholic church? At the convocation of the Ecumenical Council in 1962—certainly the most important ecclesiastical event since the Concilium Tridentinum after the Reformation—Pope John XXIII told the prelates that Catholicism might lose contact with the modern world if it remained rigidly within its authoritarian tradition. It was time, he declared, for *aggiornamento,* or for updating—which is actually a concession to the increasing army of skeptical Christians, or, as some cynics may phrase it, an attempt to calm the troubled waters in order to make possible a new and great fishing expedition. After all, Christian legend has often described the disciples as fishermen. But was the Ecumenical Council (Vatican II) really an updating?

No doubt, some progress has been made. Other religions than the Catholic were recognized as ways of men toward the divine: a Buddhist may be inspired, though the Protestants are still more or less the "erring brothers." The laity will be given more opportunities to participate in the affairs of their parish. Not long ago Catholic students were forbidden to attend purely

academic assemblies in the chapel of a nondenominational college. This has changed. No longer does the Catholic bow before
the rigid decisions of the Council of Trent of four hundred years
ago. Today, the clergy invite each other for conferences and
worship and discuss curricula. The mass is celebrated in the
vernacular. The church distinguishes between two parts of the
Bible. One part, such as the legendary stories of the Old Testament, are considered subject to human error and to the natural
limitations of the writer. The other part is still revered as divinely inspired and therefore unchangeable, such as the history
of salvation from the Jewish covenant to the bodily resurrection
of Jesus. Where is the boundary?

Nothing has been changed in the creed itself.

At the opening of the council, the pope declared that matters of dogma were not to be discussed. Indeed, if the debate
had entered into the area of creed, the Catholic church, like
the Protestant, would have found itself on a dangerous incline,
not knowing whither the road might take it. The conservative
Cardinal Ottaviani foresaw danger. If the pope had not sensed
the perils of heresy, he would not have made the surprising
move, just before the opening of the final session of the council,
to issue the encyclical *Mysterium Fidei,* a reaffirmation of the
real presence of Christ in the Eucharist, which he himself
averred to be "the most difficult part of the faith to believe."
Aparently, the mystery had caused doubt and unrest, especially
among the Catholics of the Netherlands and Germany.

Nor is it a real solution that Paul VI in his opening address
to the fourth session of the council (September 14, 1965) tried
to wash away the old sins of the church against free inquiry
by absorbing the findings of modern science into the spectrum
of religious reverence: "Him our praise of the greatness of His
glory, which has today become more evident to us because of
the advances in our knowledge of his cosmos." In spite of all
oratory, the incompatibility of dogma with empirical science
will remain. And this will increasingly disturb the educated layman as well as large segments of the Catholic clergy itself.

At a mass in the Sistine Chapel on November 17, 1966, the
pope complained that he had heard "strange and sinister re-

ports" about the spiritual slackness and worldliness of the Jesuit order, hitherto the firmest bulwark against innovation. But it was not "slackness" which characterized them; it was their intellectual and moral conscience.

On the shelves of the more educated priests one finds today books on biblical criticism. And much though they will welcome Cardinal Cushing's permission to his Boston diocese to use the Protestant Revised Standard Version of the Oxford Annotated Bible, they will nevertheless wonder why for Catholic readers fourteen notations had to be added, one of them related to the various biblical mentions of the brothers of Christ. According to the annotations, they are not really brothers but relatives. Otherwise, Holy Scripture would create confusion about the dogma of the virginity of Saint Mary.

But this is already an obsolete topic for those Catholic laymen who in various countries—often under the guidance of young and progressive priests—have formed small conventicles in which the future of the church and its dogma are discussed with utmost frankness. It is a severe challenge to their conscience to face the dilemma of whether to continue to belong to an institution, the dogmatic tenets of which they no longer accept, or whether to alter it to the degree of unrecognizability. Thus, many Catholic priests and laymen are today in the same situation as their Protestant brethren, though the latter can operate with greater freedom within their less coercive denominational framework. Nevertheless, both groups are engaged in an attempt to achieve a radical, however slow, inner rejuvenation of their church far beyond the timid concessions of the established authorities.

Historically, of course, such groups, often deeply immersed in mystical thought, have always existed. Before the Protestant Reformation, the various Cathari, the Waldenses, the Albigenses, and the Brethren of the Common Life tried to revive what they considered to be the true spirit of the Gospel. After the Reformation, various pietist sects protested against the formalism of their church. The effect of all these movements on individual souls was great; their institutional effect varied. Some disappeared for lack of sustained vitality; some were cruelly suppressed; some ended in open conflict. Similar events will happen in our time, although violent forms of oppression will generally be avoided. However, as we see in Spain, Portugal, and Ireland, there are many ways to harass an enemy.

And now two incendiary issues have been added to arouse the concern of faithful believers. One is the encyclical *Humanae Vitae* (1968), which forbids the use of contraceptives at a time when humanity may break down under the pressure of over-population. The other is the censure of the so-called Dutch Catechism, composed by a group of priests who, undoubtedly influenced by their Calvinist neighbors, have—so far as possible —tried to update the instruction of Catholic youth and laymen according to modern intellectual standards. On the advice of a special committee, the Vatican has demanded a revision of the widely spread book of instruction (November 31, 1968). Its authors—so the Vatican says—should make it unmistakably clear that the Virgin Mary "always enjoyed the honor of virginity" and that the Roman Catholic church, "infallible in doctrine and faith," must obey the pope's authority as a "supreme and universal power which the pastor of the whole Church can always freely exercise." Furthermore, the new catechism must make it clear that "God, besides this sensible world in which we live has created also a realm of pure spirits we call angels." It must leave no doubt about the fact that through the fall of Adam all mankind is born in a state of sin and that the bread and wine of the Eucharist are not mere symbols but that during the mass they are transubstantiated into "the very body and blood of Christ."

Despite all exhortations, the liberal forces released by Vatican II continue to assert themselves to a menacing degree. Even before the encyclical *Humanae Vitae* and the censuring of the Dutch Catechism, Pope Paul, on April 25, 1968, felt urged to warn an assembly of thirty thousand pilgrims in Saint Peter's Basilica, that a "whirlwind" of unauthorized ideas, advocated by extremist elements, menaced the intended "inner renewal" of the church. John XXIII, so Paul VI asserted, did not wish to change the dogma, but to find new expressions for it. Nevertheless, at a weekend meeting in Saint Louis (April 28, 1968), the National Committee on Catholic Concerns called for "a complete review" of the structure of its church. The resistance against the authority of the bishops increases in all countries; and more and more Catholic priests in Latin America speak frankly about the necessity of "Christian violence" as the only means to save the oppressed people against their rich oppressors and thus to save the Catholic church and Christianity from being identified with the forces of exploitation.

Under the continuous increase of opposition from all sides, the Hamlet-like Pope Paul VI seems to have found his way back to where he really belongs, namely, to Catholic orthodoxy. On December, 1968, he told his weekly general audience in a voice breaking with emotion that he rejects all those members of the clergy who oppose him on the issue of birth control, papal authority, priestly authority, and revised catechisms. "When it comes to its own teaching," he said, "the Church is intransigent and dogmatic—at any costs. . . . Who speaks today of Hell? This is not liked and not discussed." But if "everyone chooses the truths he likes . . . the faith disintegrates. It is no longer the faith of which St. Paul spoke." More recently, the pope has come to believe that he has discovered two main sources of "that animal barbarous and subhuman degradation" of eroticism which makes him doubt whether we still live in a society worthy of the name of "civilization."

One is Freud's psychoanalysis. Indeed, some of Freud's publications, if read by immature people, may be an invitation to moral confusion. The same can be said against Nietzsche, Goethe, Shakespeare, and especially the Bible. No great piece of literature is safe from foolish readers. But what, one may ask, was Freud's purpose but to help people to know themselves and thus to arrive at rational maturity? The other target—what an honor for him to be mentioned right beside Freud by the head of the Catholic church—is Professor Herbert Marcuse, philosopher of the New Left. His influence is already declining. Though one-sidedly analytical and sharp in his criticism of modern industrialism, Professor Marcuse is nevertheless a romantic at heart, a Rousseauist of a sort.

In the *Vatican Bulletin* the Pope declares: "In this sad phenomenon . . . we find the theory that opens the way to license, cloaked as liberty, and to the aberration of the instinct, called liberation from conventional scruples [Freud, Marcuse, etc.] [10] Who advises the pope?

Three reactions to the updating of the church are now discernible. The optimists will see the troubles of the day as the inevitable signs of the inner rebirth of the church. The day may come—so they hope—when a new and united Christianity will provide the deepest and most fertile spiritual incentive for the unity of mankind. The greatest enthusiasm can perhaps be found among Protestant clergymen, overwhelmed by the welcome they had met during the ecumenical sessions as well as by the splendor of the ceremonies at Saint Peter's (some Catholics thought there was too much of it).

The second reaction will come from a considerable number of European Catholics who believe that the church has not gone far enough in the process of liberation. They have found an eloquent interpreter in the German layman Gerd Hirschauer, author of the book *Der Katholizismus vor dem Risiko der Freiheit* (Catholicism and the Risk of Freedom).[11] The author, who calls himself a leftist in Catholic matters, emphasizes that in spite of the Vatican Council the church has not yet detached itself from its feudalistic and absolutist past and still treats its flock as a "society of minors." The Vatican decretals about the Jews and religious freedom express, according to the author, nothing but generally acknowledged facts. Some of the deepest truths of Christianity, so Hirschauer believes, have been more effectively materialized in the secular world than in the petrified church that still speaks in the mood of "dogmatic materialism" instead of inviting a real dialogue of minds.

Other skeptics, in Europe as well as in America, will remember Matthew, 7:16—"Ye shall know them by their fruits. Do men gather grapes of thorns, or figs of thistles?" Truly, many thorns and thistles still lie on the road of the Catholic church, such as the separation of Catholic children from the public school systems, the issue of mixed marriages, and the missionary work

10. *New York Times*, October 2, 1969.
11. Munich: Szcesny, 1966.

in foreign countries. Too little encouragement, many Catholic laymen think, has been given to the resolution of these problems by the clergy.

A third reaction will come from Catholic conservatives who had already warned Pope John XXIII that he would release forces that would lead to revolution. If the church gives more and more ground, even the dogma, so far upheld and venerated as God's revelation, will become the target of criticism. Will not, the conservatives may ask with good reason, such progressive measures as the celebration of the mass in the vernacular dim the magic halo in which the *sanctum* has appeared to the faithful? Certainly, the use of Latin as the universal language of the church enhanced in many participants the feeling that for their most sacred hour of worship people with hundreds of different tongues were united not only in the transcendent depth of Christian spirituality but also in its verbal expression. Latin was not just *a* language, but the *sacred language*.

What, furthermore, will the so-far forbidden reading of the Bible do to the Catholic layman? Luther's insistence on daily Bible-reading created a profound personal and individualistic form of religiosity. But it also made the thoughtful reader aware of the many contradictions contained in one of the most profound and beautiful, but also most cruel and hateful books of the world. Mainly from the Protestant camp came the movement of systematic biblical criticism that more than anything has contributed to the fact that, even in some schools of theology, the Bible has become more an object of scholarly research and literary document than a source of faith and revelation.

The growing awareness of the disintegration of the substance of Christianity, or the feeling that we no longer live in a Christian era, cannot be assuaged by reference to the fact that, according to the polls of several countries, by far the large majority of people still "believe in God." * What kind of conception of divinity and what true religious commitment would remain if one scratched the surface? Is the tolerance that now pervades the Christian folk really the result of that magnanimity of great

---

* According to a Gallup poll at the end of 1967, 97 percent of those asked whether they believed in God gave positive answers.

minds which combines deep conviction with an attempt at understanding different opinions? Or is it, as tolerance so often is, primarily a sign of waning faith, or perhaps even of fear of radical confrontation with the challenge of Christianity, such as was felt by Luther and Kierkegaard?

Moreover, so the conservative may continue, is it a sign of "taking Christianity seriously," or is it more a shift from the belief in God's inscrutable wisdom toward human politics that more and more clergymen (of all denominations) have become chairmen of social clubs or supporters of political movements? Should even the last symbol of holiness be dragged down into the noise and rattle of the market place so that a bewildered soul finds no power on earth to lift it above the worries of humanity?

To this, of course, the modernist could reply that the church, like any other institution, was always involved in secular affairs, even the most dubious ones, exactly when it claimed to speak in the name of God. If the church of Christ makes mistakes, as it surely will, the mistakes of action will be more forgivable and eventually more purifying than cowardly detachment. Jesus himself was a revolutionary who cast the money-changers out of the temple. And if rationality and enlightenment may sometimes disturb the Christian's peace of mind, thinking men will sooner find a way out of the thicket than men with blinders. Are there not still people—both Catholic and Protestant—who expect to be healed by some miracle instead of by a physician, whose old age is tortured by visions of hell, and who sell their property because they are told that the day of doom is approaching? [12]

❖   ❖   ❖

Whatever the inner dilemma of the Christian churches, they will survive because they produce better than any institution that combination of transcendental ritual, spiritual belonging, and solemn tradition which many of us need to endure the battle and the boredom of life. Both Kierkegaard and Nietzsche would have despised people who cling to a tradition they refuse

12. See John Jackson, "Two Contemporary Cults," *The Listener* (May 19, 1966).

to examine. Nevertheless, millions prefer intellectual compromise to spiritual loneliness.

On the other hand, others are searching for forms of religious organization in which they can reconcile their desire for intellectual integrity with their religious aspirations. Such organizations may still insist on being within the Christian tradition, as for example, the Unitarian Universalist Association in the United States; or they may have divorced themselves from it, as for example, the *Deutsche Unitarier* (German Unitarians), who believe that the established churches (in Germany supported by the state and by public taxation) no longer express modern man's search for truth. That which is universal in Christianity, so they hold, must be constantly rediscovered in a free dialogue with philosophy, science, and the other great religions of the world.

Other people, alienated from Western culture, find a new spiritual home in the great Asiatic faiths or in the new religious cults such as Bahai. Recently, the International Students Meditation Society has attracted a large number of students all over the world who hope to find inner enlightenment and creativeness in the Yogi art of contemplation, instead of in LSD and marihuana. All these movements emphasize the oneness of humanity because they believe that mankind participates in a universal, creative, and ever self-renewing spirit. Ralph Waldo Emerson's idea of the World Soul was one of the first American expressions of this attitude.

It may be that the very threat to eccesiastical institutions and their dogmatic tenets signifies the emergence of a new, deep, and honest concern of modern man with the mysterious forces which he will never fully comprehend by means of reason but on which, nevertheless, his existence depends.

But let those of us who enjoy the growth of the ecumenical spirit not indulge in the hope that the Catholic church will ever abandon its claim to superiority. For at the beginning of this decade (January 21, 1970), the pope reminded non-Catholic Christians, as he has done before, that Christian unity cannot come without acceptance of the primacy of the successor of Saint Peter.

2. HUMANISM

I. The Relation to the Past

In the previous chapters on humanism, we exposed ourselves to the reproach of identifying humanism more or less with a special body of knowledge, the so-called humanities. There is some justification for this, in that in Western civilization the humanist attitude resulted largely from the absorption of Greek-Roman philosophical and aesthetic values, transmitted to posterity by the ancient languages.

Actually, there is nothing in the essence of humanism that is exclusively Western. Other cultures know as well as ours that man is capable of self-transcendence, heroism, and gentleness, though he constantly has to fight dark forces in himself. They also know that man can tune himself constructively and destructively; he can be formed by persisting influences in his nation, his family, his education, and his acquaintances. Everywhere we find sayings such as: "Tell me about your friends, and I will tell you who you are."

However, much though humanism is indebted to a great and noble past, it can no longer live on it. It was too one-sidedly directed toward the contemplative values and, consequently, was predicated on a person's belonging to a privileged group—priestly, scholarly, or socially prominent. This combination of value with status existed in Hinduism, Buddhism, Confucianism, and Christianity. In these cultures the saint or the scholar-priest or the wise man stood at the top of the spiritual hierarchy, while in the Western Renaissance and in the era of Thomas Jefferson, Wilhelm von Humboldt and the Arnolds, the educated gentleman, and perhaps the creative artist, enjoyed the highest prestige. Knowledge of the ancient languages was almost indispensable. In addition, the humanist tradition suffered from the Greek prejudice, supported by the authority of Plato and Aristotle, against all manual and utilitarian work (a most welcome excuse to keep the uneducated peasant and laborer in some kind of slavery, even after the disappearance of its ancient form). Thorstein Veblen's somewhat pejorative term, "leisure class," fully applied to all groups just described in one form or another; it still survives in the liberal arts faculties of our universities. But it is rapidly disappearing as a public standard. How many of us still derive their inspiration from Plutarch and Cicero? How many can enjoy Homer and Horace, even if (or perhaps because) as pupils of old-fashioned, and now more and more disappearing classical-humanist schools, we translated them from the original (translations might have had a better effect)? If we insisted on the ideals of these schools, we would exclude almost all the leaders of modern society to whom we have referred, even a very large majority of our university professors, of whom, unfortunately, many are not even educated men, just specialists.

Thus, we should perhaps abandon the term "humanism" and replace it with—what? Here is the difficulty. We still need a name for those who differ in their view of man and the world from the Christian dualist tradition, from idealist transcendentalism, and from all other kinds of supernaturalism, on the one side, and from skepticism and nihilism on the other side, although, to a degree, they may have received important influences from all these intellectual currents. Incidentally, all of these movements have one thing in common with humanism: they, too, suffer from hazy terminology.

Just because the modern humanist is intensely interested in knowing more and more about himself he can no longer adhere to the arrogant and unscientific assumption that man can understand himself as an isolated creature. Rather, he must interpret his existence as one embedded in, nourished by, and even in his mother's womb connected with, the creative forces that govern the universe in its gigantic totality. Thus, a cosmic—in some minds, a pantheistic—strand, is woven into the mental structure of the humanist.

The humanist has no Bible, nor does he belong to any school of thought. He may not even call himself a believer in humanism or pantheism or whatever reminds him with the various isms to be found in the philosophy textbooks of the undergraduate, for all these labels bind him too narrowly to certain established modes of thinking. He always tries to extend the narrow toward the universal, in thought as well as in action.

Such a man shuns the superficial, the sloppy, and the waste inherent in pleasures devoid of depth and beauty. He is not a mere theoretician but is capable of making decisions because he prefers the risk of failure as a chance of learning, to inertia. And although he is convinced that a person who wants to be nothing but rational will be a self-righteous and unproductive bore, he hates irrationality and gladly joins those who try to extend the frontiers of experience and the intelligible even if such endeavors offend old and cherished habits of thought.

He may be persuaded that all radical thinking ends in acknowledgment of a metaphysical element in life, and he may even deepen himself through dwelling on the intuitions of the great mystics. Yet, he is everything but an obscurantist. For him there is no shortcut to wisdom.

II. The Relation to Religion

We have already touched upon the other characteristic of the modern humanist. For him the whole universe of mind, man, and nature is a continuous source of wonder—or, if one wants to say so, a revelation—though he rejects the idea of a unique and single revelation in the Judaic-Christian sense. He has, therefore, been criticized and even condemned by the established churches. As a result, the earlier humanist tradition developed not only an antiecclesiastical but often also an antireligious attitude. Even cautious minds are inclined to reject profound ideas because they find them monopolized and at the same time distorted by institutions which appeal to the desire of timid or ignorant minds for miracles and dogmatic absolutes by which they feel protected. Therefore, many humanists believe they owe it to their intellectual integrity to avoid anything that reminds them of symbols with antiquated meanings.

Furthermore, humanists are often liberals, if not Socialists and are consequently ostracized by good Christians. In the United States, public opinion is still dominated by middle-class religious conservatism.

However, all these generalizations—whether fabricated by antihumanists or humanists or by rightists or leftists—are just as confusing and preventive of the free development of our intellectual and moral future as are the labels thrown around in the marketplace of politics.

As we saw in a previous chapter, such terms as "free" or "democratic" versus "totalitarian" or "Communist" nations often obscure the view of statesmen and make it difficult for them to see possible points of mutual understanding just as, in the realm of the mind, such crude distinctions as "religious" or "theist" versus "humanist" or "atheist" can only create confusion on both sides.

Every thinking humanist will unreservedly acknowledge the religious component in man's search for a comprehensive vision of the world, for he cannot properly conceive of the human person as an isolated being. Rather, he must understand him as a receiver, participant, and contributor within an infinite and ever self-renewing order—a cosmic system. In the contemplation of this system, his mind may be imbued with a feeling of religious awe, or, out of fear of falling back into the superstitions of his ancestors, he may suppress such a feeling and thus contribute to his own mental impoverishment. Let that be his own business. But let us not build walls of separation where it would be wiser to build bridges. If he refuses to so, he is not different from the Christian who closes his mind to the more secular tradition and thus deprives himself of two privileges. First, only with some acquaintance with this tradition can he understand the development of Christian thought, because the latter is saturated with Greek-Roman philosophy. Second, he fails to make use of the human prerogative to test, to amplify, and perhaps to correct his own view of the world in the light of ideas that have given courage to great personalities, statesmen, scientists, and artists. No act invites the danger of mental stagnation more than when one cuts himself off from the many wells of inspiration that have so richly fed the stream of man's spiritual history. What else is the present crisis of the Catholic church but a desperate attempt to reconcile an overprotective dogma with the pressure of modern ideas?

III. Humanism and Optimism

There is a third point where humanism has to overcome certain dogmatic accretions of the past. It has been overoptimistic with regard to the moral potentialities of the human race. So persuasive were the hopes of the eighteenth century for a new man, freed from the fetters of dualism, feudalism and ecclesiasticism, so overwhelming the progress of science and its applications, that a wave of optimism engulfed progressive men.

But then came the cruel actuality of the nineteenth century's competitive and exploitative industrialism and the twentieth century's militaristic nationalism, already described in previous chapters. The result could only be profound disillusionment on the part of the optimists. Writers now transfer the pathologic term "schizophrenic" to the behavior of modern man and whole societies. Christianity, which was at its lowest ebb in the nineteenth century, profited from the humanist disenchantment. Its theologians, who for centuries had preached about the sinfulness of man and his need for supernatural atonement, could now say: "We told you so. Is not our doctrine that the shadow of the cross hovers over all humanity much more realistic than your idea about the perfectibility of man?"

To be sure, Christianity is more confused and more contradictory than any other system of thought, but it is still controversial. It exercises more power than it enjoys faith; it has a cult and places of worship where men can rest, even though they do not believe in the creed. On the other hand, the meeting places of humanism often resemble a university classroom where students are not particularly interested in the effusions of a professor who professes nothing because he knows that bold affirmations always involve a certain risk.

IV. Humanist Realism

Should the waning of the old humanist optimism result in the abandonment of all positive affirmations about the future of mankind?

Truly, the attainments of the human intellect have expanded to such a degree that its misuse can destroy all life on earth. Our obligation to point to the positive forces in the same intellect is that much greater. In spite of our disbelief in the rationalist and moralistic absolutes of our ancestors, there is no reason why we should allow the moral ground of humanity to be swept away. We know that very early in his existence man developed a feeling for truth and profoundness, in contrast to untruth, superficiality, and partiality. We have reason to believe that this feeling was not just a pleasant delusion but that it sprang from the desire for physical and mental survival through the establishment of an intellectual and moral order against the continual threat of undisciplined emotions and actions. The liar, the thief, and the murderer were punished not only because they had hurt some individual but out of a sense of protection of society as a whole.

To be sure, every critical observer of human culture knows that the urge for self-protection has often created highly unjust laws which served the interest, not of the whole of the population, but of dominating social classes. Taboos were held to be sacred, and illegality reigned in the guise of legality. The self-help of hungry workers—such as strikes, mass assemblies, and the formation of unions—were declared to be illegal by governments in the middle of the nineteenth century, but industrial exploitation was legal. Motivated by the conviction that there are higher laws than mere customs and that humanity had to be protected against inhumanity, humanitarian movements, earlier than most of the established churches, asked for social improvements such as minimum wages, shorter working hours, and the abolition of child labor. Humanists were in the vanguard of those who worked for prison reform, for the rights of women, and for racial equality. The worth of life on earth in its individuality and its collectivity is for the humanist the criterion against which to measure his actions. But just because of this conviction, he is also aware of the threats to human existence. Otherwise, he would be unrealistic. Much of human tragedy, so he holds, could be avoided if men were better trained to use reason. Hence his interest in education. He knows that disaster, individual and collective, inevitably occurs when stubborn reaction, timidity, and irresolution prevent innovative tendencies from realization; when adults behave like adolescents rejecting the challenge and responsibility of mature behavior; when religious organizations prejudice the minds of people against new concepts; and when whole nations close the channels of communication and prefer war to mutual understanding.

But the humanist also knows of the kind of tragedy, so profoundly illustrated by the great Greek dramatists, that jealous gods may throw man into conflicts beyond his mental and physical control. Like Oedipus, he may succumb to the wrath of demons because of the sins of his ancestors. Even children may not be spared. Because of their descendance from syphilitic or drunken parents, they may go through life as cripples. Their limbs may be mutilated because their mothers used dangerous tranquilizers. Or they may run away from home because there they met hatred instead of love or discovered that their parents, whom they would have liked to admire, were liars or criminals. Good people all over the world may become migrants even within their own nation, and young men may be caught in the dilemma between fighting an unjust war or becoming deserters.

Even in view of such situations, the humanist believes that foresight might have prevented what at first glance may look like fate going amok. Thus he has much in common with the existentialist's distrust of cloudy idealisms as well as with the relativist's conviction of the dependence of human thought and conduct on changing conditions. He refuses to glorify life as a continuous blessing or to believe in a "dear God," busy helping men pull cars out of the ditches into which they have driven them. But he also refuses to concentrate on misery and evil. Like the great Stoic philosophers of antiquity, he looks for balance. Both excessive optimism and pessimism reveal a lack of inner equilibrium. While the optimist may have the courage of initiative, persistent pessimism is sterile.

V. Humanist Ethics

Since the humanist believes that despite his dependence on natural forces man is given a degree of freedom in forming his life, where can he find valid directions for his conduct? In earlier times he relied on divine commandments, though more often than not he did not and could not obey them. The Sermon on the Mount is one of the profoundest expressions of the human desire for purity for and union with God. It contains one of the most inspired and inspiring prayers of mankind, the first part being cosmological, the second part existential. But for the most part, Jesus's exhortations and the accompanying threats are unrealistic.

Which ideas, then, should the humanist cultivate in order to lift his conscience to a level where he can unite his desire for realism and intellectual honesty with his urge for attaining a world view more comprehensive and satisfactory than factual knowledge and moral precepts?

First, the humanist must develop the quality of empathy, or the capacity of projecting himself into the feeling and spirit of other persons. He cannot help but regard himself as a participant in the endlessly sad and joyful experiences of the human race as a whole. The religious notion that every person is responsible for the totality of humanity is not foreign to him, especially as he feels not only the virtues but also the errors which are potentially inherent in his deeper self. This sense of empathic responsibility, as we may call it, extends from the human world into the world of nature. He hates the ruthless destruction of trees and the extinction of helpless species of animals as much as the exploitation of children, which still goes on in many countries.

Second, the humanist believes that, if there is any hope for the moral future of the race, it will come from the right understanding and application of the scientific method. As a matter of fact, as far as man is concerned, it began with the Socratic admonition of "Know thyself." ("The unexamined life is not worth living.") Enjoy the power of your will and your emotions, but be also honest—be a kind of scientific inquirer in the examination of your motives. Do not reward yourself for deeds, even good ones, you have done out of self-interest.

But in order to answer more fully the quest for a humanist ethics, we have to go beyond the science, or the art, of self-knowledge and its moral ramifications, into that area of human activity which today is understood as science in the proper sense of the term. This activity, however, must not be understood as a mere technique. Rather, it must be understood as a ceaseless attempt to create a universe of order out of a mass of fragmented prehensions, whether they belong to the realm of nature or to the realm of man. Hence, any systematic research into the genesis and quality of human culture, such as anthropology, psychoanalysis, history, education, or the behavioral sciences in the widest sense of the term, will be welcomed by the humanist.

On the other hand, the humanist cannot admire the specialist in a narrow branch of knowledge if he never asks himself *why* there can be such a human pursuit as science and for what purposes it will be used. Still less he sympathizes with high school or college teachers of science who, merely for didactic purposes, perform cruel experiments with helpless animals, knowing well that their repetitive work contributes nothing to the advancement of human knowledge.

To phrase it in other terms: The very concept of science is for the humanist too wide and ever changing to yield a dogma. That which was scientific truth a hundred years ago is error today. Our experimentalists can no longer consult the notes and textbooks of their college years. Science is not only a continuous process of learning but also of unlearning.

Yet, though the good scientist knows that he will never possess the ultimate truth, he has been inspired by the idea of the pursuit of truth—by the unswerving will to examine, to reexamine, and to correct even those of his discoveries of which he was proud if his colleagues come up with better solutions. The scientist needs the virtue of patience that springs from the still deeper virtue of selfless devotion. The truly scientific person forgets himself because he knows that he works within an ever greater and encompassing order that cannot be defined but only intuited. Yet, its presence can be observed in every state of evolution, from the slightest particle to the most distant galaxy. There comes to mind the ancient myth of Phoenix, the bird ever born out of its own ashes, or Goethe's dictum, "*Stirb und werden*" (Die and become).

A deep sense of wonder emerges. Here is our little mind, working by means of the brain. What are the mind and brain compared with the world's incomprehensible magnitude? Yet, at one point this brain, growing three times as great in size as that of its nearest rival, the chimpanzee, did something totally unique in the history of our universe, as far as we know. It began to reflect on the being that housed it in his head, on his environment, on his birth and death, on the tasks he had to perform during the short span of his life, and on the powers that reigned over it. Man invented the art of language and of playing in forms different from the play of puppies. Whereas the play of young animals, however enchanting, remains an end in itself, with some vestiges persisting in the adult, the play of man contains the germs of imagination, of myth, and of art. Probably most of man's creative ideas, even in seemingly distant fields, have their origin in play. "Man is man only and wholly when he plays," says Friedrich Schiller in his *Letters on Aesthetic Education.*

A person must be dull to the wonders of the human mind not to see the challenges and potentialities which the pursuit of science, as we defined it, contains in regard to the moral problem. Certainly, many individuals are unable to transfer the quality of the operations in which they are engaged during their occupational hours to their moral conscience and conduct. A tax consultant who meticulously goes through the accounts of his client, may himself cheat; a brave soldier may be a coward in his civil life; pious folks may lie, or a clergyman may look with indifference at the misery of the poor and the exploited. And among the scientifically minded, there will be many who are unable or unwilling to fuse the order they discover in their work with a corresponding order in their daily lives. Often it is the people who work with their hands, the smiths and the carpenters, whose personalities identify with the character of their activities, for they experience day by day that a sloppily made piece of handicraft breaks down, whereas it may be decades before fallacious philosophical theories show their fatal effect on the history of man.

However, we may assume that in the search for knowledge, through the patience, the humility, and the sense of reverential wonder for the cosmic order—unfathomable yet revealing itself in the minutest phenomena of life—we have, besides responsible empathy, the germs of an ethic which is natural but which at the same time transcends the boundaries of the tangible, leaving room for the ever expanding imaginations of the mind. But are we not here dealing with an esoteric culture that is accessible only to a very few privileged men, just as was the case with the humanism of the Greek philosophers, the Renaissance, the Humboldts, and the Arnolds?

Indeed, this book will never conceal the author's conviction that truly eminent and productive qualities are not sown in the earth like the seeds of dandelions. Those who possess these qualities are rare and often desperately lonely. Nevertheless, they have disciples; gradually their ideas and ideals spread from the few to the many. So it was with Christianity, as with every religion. And so it will be with the idea of the unity of mankind.

But there is one difference between a rational culture, based on observation and interpretation of the observed, and those cultures which mingle the wisdom they may contain with magical elements. Whereas magical cultures are possessive, dominating, and conclusive, rational cultures try to help their believers to arrive at that mature attitude of mind which combines direction with self-correction, realism with faith, observation with intuition, and world immanence with the courage of admitting the ultimately mystical character of being. What is it? Why is it? For what is it? These questions we will never answer. Yet those who never ask them are ignorant of the great critical questions of life, while those who take resort to comfortable, though obsolete, traditions become the prisoners of the past.

There is a further difference between the old classical and the modern humanism. Our present society is no longer hierarchical, visionary, and romantic. Rather, it is saturated with critical and empirical thinking. Unless one is conditioned from infancy to believe in rituals presented to him as divinely revealed and necessary for his salvation, even an intelligent high school graduate is reluctant to accept ideas based on faith beyond proof. Mere historical arguments do not impress him, for he knows of change. But he is willing to follow thought even into metaphysics if the chain of thought is anchored in the physical realm. The same is the case with the modern worker or farmer. He is more sophisticated mechanically than many college graduates a hundred years ago, because he uses machines, reads about new inventions, and sees astronauts on television. Like a sensitive youth, many of them speculate about the nature of man and the world, though mostly without adequate guidance. The schools through which they went may have taught them a modicum of science, just enough to make them suspicious of vague abstractions, but not enough to prepare them for placing the shattered pieces of information into a meaningful whole. Nor can the churches do it, for they begin at the wrong end and are tangled in the web of mythological concepts. Some of them may contain the profoundest intuitions of the human race, but they have become incomprehensible to men who spend most of the day away from nature, in factories or in the seats of bulldozers.

One last point. When we look at the eight thousand years or so through which we can observe the development of civilization, from the painter of the caves of Lascaux to our modern artists (who have more in common than is generally assumed), it seems that man is fundamentally a mystic. Many errors, detours, and superstitions, as well as jealousies and persecutions—all in the name of the holy—have accrued from this mystical urge. Yet, man cannot help asking what is behind the visible, how he can relate his life to the encompassing force, and whether this force listens to his entreaties.

But how can this desire for a vertical direction in our existence find expression in a technological age? Many of us will say: "Go into the woods and listen to their silence. Look at the stars. Read great poetry, hear music, contemplate the interflow between form, color, design, and meaning in a painting." Everything is available. A housewife can listen to Bach while cooking, and a Beethoven symphony may accompany her quarrels with her angry husband. Museums are open, and exotic landscapes can be seen on the screen. But the sense of the extraordinary that artistic creations and the grandeur of nature should create—how many feel it, just because it can so easily be bought?

Thus, many Catholics go to mass though they do not believe in the miracle of transubstantiation, and Protestants tolerate the sermons of their ministers only because they like the beautiful hymns. Yet, they will avoid thinking about the meaning of it all. If they did think and speak about it with their wives, children, and critical friends, doubts could arise and peace of mind vanish.

More and more honest people renounce even this last refuge of inner security. In many towns all over the world old sacred buildings turn into ruins or are loaned for commercial purposes. At the same time a number of so-called unbelievers who would like to have a place for free and undogmatic worship are homeless. Their unfulfilled desire for some kind of solemnity in a world of platitudes is a much greater predicament of modern civilization than we are aware of, for it works mostly in the subconscious regions of the mind. People miss something precious, though they do not know what it is. Even Protestant churches, which claim to represent Christianity in its originality more than Catholicism, try to escape the predominance of verbal concepts which no longer carry the same intensity of feelings as during the time of Luther and Calvin.

As the result of the ecumenical movement, churches are now used for interdenominational worship. Thus, like Plato in the *Republic*, we may indulge in daydreaming. Will the time come when these buildings will be used also by non-Christian groups desirous of the experience of spiritual community?

Christianity is anchored in a great past, expressed in inimitable works of symbolic beauty, whereas the new "sects," as they are often called condescendingly, lack the visible luster of ancient ancestry, though they may be motivated by ideas older than Christianity—ideas to be found in Hinduism, Buddhism, Taoism, and pantheistic mythologies. The Christian Church Fathers themselves mingled together Judaism, Platonism, Aristotelianism, Stoicism, and old pagan rituals.

Unfortunately, our time is no longer capable of creating profound and pregnant symbols. What we try in this respect seems artificial. It is appalling to think that the last symbol that impressed the masses was the swastika of Hitler. He saw it first above the entrance of a church in his native Braunau. As the image of celestial movements, it appears in Hinduism and among American Indians. Thus, even the National Socialist swastika is not new; it is only the most diabolic distortion of something sacred—a kind of modern witchcraft.

The lack of artistic-symbolic creativeness explains why some modern movements, begun with prophetic enthusiasm, soon stall or degenerate into discussion clubs or even into shelters for mentally estranged people, unable to cope with the demands of society.

The failure of these modern movements to express their spiritual intentions is revealed, to use but one example, in their incapacity to create a genuine architectural style. No doubt, in some few cases they have marvelously succeeded, but mostly they have created edifices which without much imagination could be changed into an exclusive country club with a comfortable bar. The same also holds true of Catholic and Protestant churches and Jewish temples paid for by congregations that no longer believe in the attractiveness of their old symbols and want to be modern. They may even prefer jazz rhythms to Palestrina or Bach, for the simple reason that the music of the latter have lost relevance.

Sophisticated and wealthy Americans who have contributed to these modern buildings remember some European cathedrals, or perhaps an old village church in Italy or the Alps, where they felt surrounded by a previously unknown though eloquent silence, serene tranquillity, and inner freedom. Or they may find these virtues in a Japanese garden arranged according to Zen principles of contemplation. Why has Zen suddenly become a movement among intellectual westerners, though it is well-nigh impossible to transplant intimate atmospheres from one culture to another?

Two obstacles stand in the way of the expansion of Christian ecumenism to what one might call "universal ecumenism." First, the secular minds may be afraid of intellectually dishonest compromises when they assemble in halls with saints in the niches and the cross on the altar. They do not have enough imagination and understanding of the myth-building quality in man all over the earth, though it expresses itself on different levels of rationality. They fail to realize that even their own attempts to formulate a Weltanschauung are dependent on the spirit of their time. To a superior mind, even our modern scientific systems are myths.

On the traditional side, millions of Christians and their clergy will be afraid of desecrating the sacred if they offer their houses of worship to "disbelievers." They fail to remember the words of the founder of their own religion: "In my father's house are many mansions."

Thus, with both sides not yet ready for the creation of a spiritual continuum, we will go on living and thinking with such totally antiquated and divisive categories as the religious and the secular, the believers and the disbelievers, the idealists and the materialists, and all that stuffy vocabulary, cherished by insecure minds that feel safer behind secluding walls than in a house with open doors and windows.

We are today in a state of history when society will either break into more and more spiritual fragments or will succeed in finding a synthesis between the rational-empirical conscience on the one hand, and, on the other hand, the urge for comprehensive visions of life. These visions can be expressed only in an intuitive form which transcends the visible. But though they are mystical in the profoundest sense of the term (as is everything that reaches toward the ultimate), they must not be obscurantist escapes from critical thinking. One without the other —mere rationality as much as undisciplined imagination—will lead to impoverishment, however great the riches of science and technology. It will not only continue our mental malaise but will also finally lead to social and international disaster, for only heathy minds can make healthy politics.

But let us not indulge in the kind of despondency which lacks historical perspective. The number of the really concerned has always been smaller than the number of the unconcerned. How poor was the mental life of the village population and even of the craftsmen two hundred years ago! How widespread were pestilence and starvation!

We cannot say that the moral conduct of man has improved since the days of the first lawgivers of the ancient civilizations. Often when nobody expects it the beast in man breaks out in violent rages. Yet, we have become more sensitive, immensely richer in experience, and more skilled in the use of instruments and the mastery of nature. This is the reason why we are also more bewildered and exposed to temptations. But our moral responsibilities are greater also. As we have seen in earlier chapters, these responsibilities are no longer limited to the family, the neighbor, and the nation, but are extended to mankind as a whole. That means that in order to act more ethically, we have also to know more than our forebears in their regional surroundings. Ignorance is no longer merely an individual shortcoming; it is a human calamity.

Hence, whatever the humanist's answer to the riddle of existence, at the basis of every answer must be the attempt to know as much as possible about man, his origin, his mind, his endeavors, his failures, and his potentialities.

3. EDUCATION

Education is an art whereby one person helps another person to become more informed, more rational, more aware of his social obligations, inherently richer, or capable of lifting himself above a state of nature toward a state of culture.

As in every social situation, so in education the step from simpler to wider and more complicated conditions of existence generates crises, for the new challenges the old forms of living and thinking. For the courageous, such challenge increases the zest of life, whereas it is a source of fear to the timid, who refuse to admit the kinship between man, choice, and change.

Even among the primitives, dissidents must have emerged who were torn by conflicting tendencies. The tribe demanded loyalty to its customs and idols, but, necessary though they were for survival, they also blocked the way toward new and rewarding ventures. The more advanced a culture, the more it creates alternatives and the necessity for decisions, which in turn create new vistas. Every door leads to another door. Stability gives way to mobility, authority to criticism, and evolution may change into revolution.

It is a mark of a healthy society that even in a period of transition it does not carelessly abandon old loyalties unless they have lost their meaning. Rather, it cleanses them of their historical accidents and incorporates their human essence into the new scheme of living where they may prove their intrinsic value more vigorously than before. In other words, a healthy society is both conservative and progressive. And so is a healthy school system.

Impermanence and permanence go together in human civilization. We no longer wish to live in the old Greek city-states, but we still live with Greek thought and art. If a culture tears its roots out of the past, it will wither like a plant without earth. A world traveler who no longer knows a place where he can rest, renew himself, and transform fleeting impressions into new intimacies, is a permanent refugee. Here is the challenge to education in our time of transition. It has to root young minds in the past and at the same time encourage them to prepare for change; it has to give them the sense of continuity and at the same time the courage to try the new.

In this attempt, educators have to realize that schools are but one of many socializing agencies. In the flux of days, we are rarely conscious of the multitude of influences which form our habits, judgments, and prejudices. The more imperceptible they are, the more powerful they may be. In driving our car as in forming our lives, the hidden dangers are the worst. The first five years of life, so psychologists tell us in perhaps too deterministic a mood, fix our character traits. We are affected by our community, its streets, buildings and entertainments; by our work, our friends; and by the innumerable casual conversations down to the chatter of more or less joyfully attended cocktail parties.

We have already spoken of the close alliance between education and statecraft. Retardation in education engenders retardation in the life of nations and vice versa. Through his instruction before the blackboard and as a guide of youth, the teacher will either help political reactionaries or will help progressive statesmen in the fulfillment of the urgent historical tasks of the present, as we have described them in the chapter on the state. In the arena of the conflicts between constructive ideas and obsolete conventions, the teacher will be particularly confronted with the following problems:

(1) *Dogmatic World Views.* Such views claim to have their origin in sacred revelations or social taboos and extend their influence into many areas of life—moral, political, ethic, and ethnic. In spite of our secular culture, they still divide the people of most modern countries with regard to religious instruction in schools, and they hamper the free discussion of essential human problems among teachers and students. We have touched on these problems in various chapters, especially in those on religion and humanism.

(2) *Nationalist Sentiment.* There is not much need to examine in detail the influence of this quality on modern education. To be sure, one of the basic elements in the political education of youth should be patriotism, or man's love for his country and its culture. But this love should not prevent him from realizing that we live in a transition from nationalist isolation to internationalist cooperation.

The new community toward which we are aiming requires men capable of making a synthesis between the natural desire to be somewhere at home and, on the other hand, the desire to understand the world at large with all its historical and cultural differences. To create such an understanding will not be easy. Today the nation is a reality that reminds us of home, landscape, taxes, and political and military duties, while the idea of mankind as a unity remains in the verbal sphere. Despite the proliferation of international institutions, this idea lacks the warmth and the felt concreteness that engenders a lasting sense of obligation. The flag of the United Nations has by no means the same symbolic value for the French or for the Americans as their national banners do. Not long ago, school boards in California forbade the mentioning of the United Nations and of UNESCO in history classes, and several colleges prevented the discussion of socialism and communism, as if ignorance had ever been an effective means of defense.

The aversion of a certain type of people against the idea of a transnationalist period of history stems not only from the usual fear of the new. More people than we suppose suffer from a mostly unconscious anxiety that a world of peace might offer them no outlet for their aggressiveness. It will depend on one's opinion about psychoanalytical theories whether one wants to explain aggressive behavior as motivated by the "death instinct," which from time immemorial has driven man into suicidal actions. But it is certain that many people do not want to be deprived of their chance to display their superiority and to fight somebody. Their mental poverty allows them to see only one alternative to boredom—the excitement of contest—although, like the typical football or boxing fan, they often prefer vicarious to direct participation in the battle. Moreover, whole industries and highly respected professions are working today in the service of nationalist interests. The outbreak of peace would destroy their profit. But as William James has partly shown in his famous essay "The Moral Equivalent of War,"[13] man has many ways to divert aggressiveness into healthy channels. He can engage in sport and explorations; he can combat poverty and prejudice; he can devote himself to political service. Man is a fighting but also a loving animal. It is the mission of education to convert the energy of the fighting spirit into the spirit of cooperation.[14] The Peace Corps is just the beginning.

13. New York: American Association for International Conciliation, 1910.

14. Many books have recently been written about the manner in which certain animal species disarm their aggressive instinct. See especially Konrad Lorenz, *On Aggression* (New York: Harcourt, Brace, 1963). On the general problem of war, aggressiveness, and peace see Sande Pulley, *World Citizen or World War. A Plea for Universal Consciousness* (New York: Exposition Press, 1967).

(3) *The Rebellion of Youth.* Surely, so we proclaim in our commencement address, the growing person should be aware of his individuality and uniqueness. He should make his own choices and be able to say no, which is often more difficult to say than yes. He should distrust cheap and prejudiced opinions and resist the pressure of authorities in which he does not believe. In other words, a young person who leaves our schools should have the strength to become an "authentic" person. But if he returns from school with ideas contrary to those of his father, the latter accuses the teacher of spreading subversive opinions.

The present conflict of generations is often connected with the movement of the Socialist "hippies." Their critics point at the infantile behavior of some of them, at their attempt to hide their insecurity behind vanity of the unwashed bohemian, and at their sexual experiments.

But we should not forget that hippies represent only the extreme. They are the crest of much deeper waves of unrest. The best of our youth are torn by conflict. They may collide with their parents, thus repeating the collisions that have occurred in every generation. Today, however, many youths just refuse to cooperate with a culture they consider to be rotten.

Modern youth is afraid that after all its education it will suffocate in monotonous and meaningless work. It despairs of the capacity of our culture to create human ends which make a person free and authentic. It is searching for authority in which it can believe, but it does not find it. Instead of receiving guidance and inspiration, it discovers viciousness and hypocrisy that often hide under the names of patriotism, morality, and civilization. Whereas at the beginning of this century protesting youth moveemnts were "Rousseauist" *(retournez à la nature)*, many young men and women in our big cities do not have a chance to refresh themselves through contact with fresh rivers and mountains. They are too far away, and a car is too expensive. Great is, under these circumstances, the temptation of taking a "trip" on the magic carpet of LSD! Thus, the serious young men in our universities tend to break out of a society that, in their opinion, demands something like the obedience of sailors subject to the will of an insane captain. They prefer mutiny to submission, though they may not know where to sail after the captain has been thrown overboard.

As we have already indicated in an earlier chapter, democracy has lost its "metaphysics." The older a student becomes, the more inclined he is to believe that politics is just a kind of bargaining. He also learns that for decades the American republic has supported throughout the world more antidemocratic and progressive governments. To be sure, the Vietnam war is not the only event that has incited student rebellions. Other nations have had them too. But certainly it is one of the main contributors to that frightening political and moral disillusionment which pervades the United States.

Yet it is not only a changing culture, bewildered or lazy parents, or a mistaken education responsible for so many young men and women entangled in a net of rebellion and aimlessness, of expectation and frustration, of drug and sex adventures, and of doubt and cynicism. Certain things are not easy but require effort. This applies not merely to ownership or knowledge or influence but even more so to the deepest delights of life, such as love, the enjoyment of art, even the enjoyment of nature. Too many of our youth no longer want to make this effort. They refuse to wait (being able to wait, is according to Lao-tzu, the distinctive quality of man). They do not intend to climb in order to arrive at the summit. Just as through television the rarest and farthest is within easy reach, so it should also be in reality. But just because they shun the difficult, they deprive themselves of the depths of life. The exciting, then, should take its place, but it never is a substitute for the lasting satisfactions that make existence worthwhile. For nervousness is no surrogate for steady endeavor.

In all historical intervals between authority lost and new authority gained, or oppression on one side and unorganized opposition on the other, despair and unrest exploded in wild outbreaks such as the destruction of machines in the centers of early industrialism, or the revolts of the German weavers when English imports lowered prices so much that people were forced to live below the subsistence level. There appeared clandestine attempts to overthrow the whole existing order, or prophets with vague visions of social perfection, either in the form of religious millennialism, political utopianism, or atheist anarchism. They were bitterly or ironically fought by Marx, Engels, and their followers, as a primitive and ineffective form of revolution.

Today, in certain parts of the world we are headed toward new revolts, such as the riots in modern slums or the assassinations of John F. Kennedy and Martin Luther King, executed by disturbed individuals who nevertheless—so many believe—acted at the behest of political enemies. The deep defects in our technological order (or "disorder") reveal themselves also in a new kind of anarchism. In England alone, the anarchist newspaper *Freedom*, the anarchistically inclined *Delphic Review*, and the *University Libertarian* are being published. Anarchist influences can also be felt in the writings of Aldous Huxley, Sir Herbert Read, and George Orwell—all three frightened by the loss of humanity in our technological mechanisms.

Whereas the nineteenth century's Socialist or anarchist movements, though sometimes started by educated and privileged persons, were addressed to the large and suffering masses, modern anarchism is largely individualistic and aristocratic. Its adherents, often coming from educated families, want to save the uniqueness of the human individual against its archenemy of modern mass organization and mass equalization, represented primarily by the modern state. They have read Nietzsche's condemnation of this monster in his *Zarathustra:*

> Somewhere there are still peoples and herds, but not with us, my brethren: with us there are states.
>
> The state? What is that? Well! now open your ears, for now I deliver my sentence on the death of people.
>
> The state is called the coldest of all cold monsters. And coldly it lies; and this lie creepeth out of its mouth: "I, the state, am the people."
>
> It is a lie. Creators they were who created the peoples and hung one belief and one life over them; thus they served life.
>
> Destroyers they are who lay traps for many, calling

them the state; they hung a sword and a hundred desires over them.[15]

(4) *Controversial Topics.* What, now, can the schools do
within their own precincts to prepare youth for constructive
living in a time of dissension? It wold be unfortunate if they
assumed a role of passivity, as reactionary groups would like
them to do. First, without offense to any decently defensible
opinion on the part of the parents, the teacher in the kinder-
garten and the elementary school can provide experiences that
are conducive to the idea of national unity and the elimination
of dangerous prejudices. Generally, the young are more open
to social toleration than the adult.[16] In high school the teacher
of history and the social sciences can invite the young mind to
investigate the relationship between cause and effect in human
affairs, war and peace, the rise of decline of cultures, or ideals
and actions in the life of nations. A wise guide of youth can
teach the art of judgment with regard to the social problems
of the community and at the same time defend himself against
the wrath of self-seeking businessmen. Certainly, up to the years
of adolescence the schools of a nation should be mainly places
where the young—without being narrowly indoctrinated—are
inducted into their culture. They should be provided with the
maps for social orientation and be shown how to read them.

However, much more than the preparatory schools, higher
education (if the term "higher" still has any meaning) should
provide the opportunity for free and courageous discussion of
even the most troubling problems. If those who are being prepared for leading positions are unprepared for controversy,
where will they learn to meet it? The blind, then, will lead the
blind. Those who want to avoid their first sleepless nights after

15. "Of the New Idol," in Part I of *Thus Spake Zarathustra.* Translated by Alexander Tille (New York: Macmillan, 1896), p. 62.
16. See Barbara Biber, "Preschool Education," in *Education and the
Idea of Mankind,* ed. Robert Ulich (New York: Harcourt, Brace, 1966),
p. 71-96.

being shaken out of cherished prejudices should not populate colleges and universities. We have to educate men and women who know what is worth knowing but who are, at the same time, willing to question what they know. Only through continuous openness to new ideas and their applications can a culture be saved from disruptive discontinuity.

Therefore, in order to be competent, our teachers must have learned the art of evolutionary thinking. Have we a sufficient number of such teachers, and is their profession sufficiently attractive to give it their loyalty? Until the end of the nineteenth century—except those in the universities—teachers were miserably paid, enjoyed little social prestige and freedom of action, and had to obey orders from above. Only the instructors in the old classical schools were, so to speak, esteemed as gentlemen. This has changed, or, we should say, is changing. But much remains to be done.

Even textbooks used by advanced nations tend to stifle the curiosity of the young and to relate their learning one-sidedly to the existing situation rather than to the demands of the future. The prejudices of middle-class adults still weigh heavily upon our schools.

In older times, the young gentleman was sent on a grand tour to widen his knowledge of the world, or he was sent as an officer to the colonies. Unfortunately, traveling is still a privilege of a few, often of those who profit little from it. However, modern governments, universities, and schools have now made the exchange of students and scholars easier than in earlier times. But even without traveling, we can include comparative aspects in the curriculum, especially in such subjects as biology, anthropology, and the social sciences. In history classes teachers can show their students how other cultures have developed and why they did so, that history proceeds on different levels of development, and that a "lower" level is not necessarily inferior to a "higher." How would the world look to us, we might ask, if for a while we forgot our own criteria of progress and used instead the criteria of an Indian Guru, who sees his ancient culture drowned in the waves of Western civilization which he might regard as a medley of Christianity, political ideologies, technology, and highly organized barbarism.[17]

"More important than any single policy decision that we might make is the strengthening of our capacity to reconsider established policies in the light of changing facts and circumstances." So wrote Senator Fulbright in the *Bulletin of the Atomic Scientists* of June, 1966. His article deals especially with higher education, the highest purpose of which he sees in "the enrichment of the life of the individual and advancement of the eternal effort to bring reason and justice and humanity into the relations of men and nations." Senator Fulbright would certainly agree that our universitaies could not get far in the pursuit of their cultural mission unless well-prepared young men and women entered through their doors.

(5) *Creativity, or the Few and the Many.* These considerations lead us to a further responsibility of education, the discovery and cultivation of talent, or the *fostering and support of creativity*. When danger threatens a society, the salvation always lies in the emergence of a few who understand the warning voice of history, acknowledge the necessity of change, and transform the fear into a sense of challenge. When, as at the end of antiquity, such men fail to arise, or, so far as they exist, are not supported by their contemporaries, decay is imminent. Therefore, even at the risk of some detour into subtle psychological problems, we will discuss the characteristics of the creative personality,[18] for unless the schools are able to recognize it in time and to stimulate it, they kill the most precious elements in their society. How often have they done so!

17. See in this connection: *Education for World Responsibility*, U.S. Department of State (Government Printing Office: Washington, D.C., 1966), and the various publications under the auspices of the Council for the Study of Mankind: *Education and the Idea of Mankind*, ed. Robert Ulich (New York: Harcourt, Brace, 1964); *Economics and the Idea of Mankind*, ed. Bert F. Hoselitz (New York: Columbia University Press, 1965).

18. On the subject of creativity, see especially *Explorations in Creativity*, ed. Ross Money and Teher Razik (New York: Harper and Row, 1967). See also Robert Ulich, "On Creativity," in *The University and the New World*, York University (Toronto: University of Toronto Press, 1962).

At least seven rather general characteristics distinguish the creative, from the average, personality. They are so interwoven that they defy any attempt at sharp separation; yet, our conceptual language has no other means to elucidate the complex but to illuminate the parts.

First, the creative person possesses a high degree of *spontaneity*, an inner energy drives him forward. We hope modern research will tell us more about this quality in the future, for the relation between mental phenomena and the chemistry of the body is no longer the secret it was twenty years ago. We also know that the gift of creative spontaneity, though ultimately outside our will, can be cultivated through exercise and endurance. The enduring strength of the genius, however, is not that of an athlete. Many great men lived in a fragile frame. The German poet Friedrich Schiller protested his many sicknesses with the obstinate words: "It is the soul that builds itself the body" (*"Es ist der Geist, der sich den Körper baut"*).

And so might have said Erasmus of Rotterdam, Blaise Pascal, Elizabeth Barrett Browning, Charles Steinmetz, and Eve Curie. They all are paradigms of that interaction between psyche and soma which, under the influence of mechanical concepts of science, we have neglected for a long time but about which the ancient Indians already had profound intuitions.

The spontaneity of a creative person is enhanced by his second quality, that of *sensitivity*. Both spontaneity and sensitivity are like fine edges by virtue of which the mind cuts into the dim mass of the unknown. In many languages, all those words which denote sharpness and its antonym, bluntness, have metaphorical meaning. We speak of a "sharp" and "incisive" intellect and of a "dull" and "blunt" mind. Like spontaneity, sensitivity is in no way a passive response to the stimuli of the environment. The physical organs that connect us with the outer world—the ear that hears, the eye that sees, and the skin that reacts to touch—are not merely receivers. They work only because of their interaction with a marvelously developed nerve and brain system. Therefore, any comparison with mechanical instruments, such as radar or a computer, or with the sensitiveness of animals (which in many species is, in particular respects, higher than ours) is fallacious, because in man impressions received from outside or from within can be transformed into questions and the questions into concepts.

How this transformation of prehensions into concepts and meanings comes about, or how unconscious life changes into self-conscious and even self-critical life, is one of the great riddles of evolution. We do not know what thinking is.

Whenever sensitivity passes from mere sensory impressions into more lasting experiences, it is accompanied by emotions, just as air blown into a flute is accompanied by a tone. We can be deeply moved also by nature, but except in cases of insanity all human existence is primarily interhuman existence—all personal life is interpersonal life—and such life is either sympathetic and cooperative, hostile or loveless, or lived in an atmosphere of brute apathy, which is the worst type of life.

The high degree of sensitivity characteristic of the creative mind renders its possessor highly susceptible to the plenitude of tragic and often unkind human events. His experiences refuse to remain on the surface; they may cut deeply into his soul. Instead of dismissing them lightly, he dwells upon them with intense joy and love or with intense sorrow and despair. His world is richer for this reason, but it is also more fraught with danger. He may be irritable and inclined toward depressive moods.

How—this is our third question—can the creative individual defend himself against himself? Only through a heightened degree of *self-discipline* that teaches him to conserve his energy for purposes conducive to his further development. He is too rich to be a moralist, but he does not dissipate himself. Conscious of his own value and of the value of every member of humanity, he maintains his integrity in the midst of inner and outer turbulence. He may be overwhelmed by passion, because there is a deep connection between creativity and excitability—perhaps also sexuality. But his urge toward form and meaningful expression will turn even failure and immorality into productivity. If it were not for the great "sinners" from Saint Augustine to Rousseau, Goethe, Balzac, and Wilde, man would be more ignorant about himself than he is.

From disciplined reflection on the value of experience the creative person develops, as his fourth outstanding quality, a sense of *purposefulness*. Whereas most people are pushed by concatenations of external circumstances (outer directed, as one says today), the creative person creates his own goal. He rigorously rejects that which does not fit into the curve of his life. Only assimilable impressions are retained. Thus, the paradox emerges that the genius—known to be excitable, bounteous, and overgenerous—is at the same time a careful steward of his talent.

These considerations force upon us a fifth distinction of the creative mind: *imagination, intuition, or inventiveness* (the three terms may be used interchangeably). He reaches beyond the immediate and obvious to arrive at insights closed to ordinary men, because more than others he senses the inner kinship between all things existing—hence the astounding ease and wealth of his associations, of his metaphorical thinking and language, irrespective of whether he speaks as a statesman, a scholar, or an artist.

To be sure, everyone who thinks within wide circles shows some degree of imagination. However, in the spontaneous and sensitive individual imagination assumes a degree of unusual intensity and suddeness of result. It is a gift that comes from inner spheres—rich, turbulent and often nebulous in their state of birth. They lie below the level of analytical thinking. Although imagination can be cultivated to a degree, it cannot be commanded. All mental acts have something enigmatic about them, but the intuitional are most enigmatic of all.

An aesthetic component works in all intuitiveness that can best be illustrated by reference to the work of the artist. According to common opinion, the artist belongs to the eminently intuitive types, consequently, more than other mortals he is susceptible to the ever changing facets of life. Fascinated by the charm, the color, and the form of men and things, he easily falls prey to contradictory moods. He is considered to be careless about conventions and money and to be more impulsive than reliable in his political opinions.

But the frequent notion of the artist as a kind of bohemian is one-sided. It fails to see that the artist pays for his sensitivity by his exposure to the heights and abysses of experience and by their often tortuous transformation into a finished work, admired by his contemporaries, or perhaps rejected until later generations awaken to it. Like Dante in the *Divine Comedy*, he may pass from limbo to hell and not even have a Virgil as his mentor. And while Dante finally arrives at heaven, many an artist will not. On the battlefield of life, the genius is alone—as Dante was himself—if only for the reason that he is ahead of others.

But intuition is not merely a form of quick apprehension of the unknown and unformed or a sudden feeling of release from pent-up tensions and emotions. In order to be creative, intuition needs a built-in structure, or "logic," which is the result of mental discipline. It may be felt or not felt during the creative act, but it must nevertheless be there. A mere brainstorm is not an intuition. Only to the mind endowed with the virtue of order will the deeper orders of life open their gates.

The gift of intuition is in no way the monopoly of the artist. It is present whenever new light appears on the horizons of humanity, in religion, in philosophy, in science, and in the fields of action. No doubt, the scholar has to follow rigorous methods of inquiry, but in order to be more than descriptive, or analytical, he also needs the gift of inventiveness. Each new step in the art of inquiry results from a mixture of knowledge, meticulousness, and intuition. Quantitatively speaking, the scholar of genius may not know more than his equally learned contemporaries, but he is able to use the known as a springboard to the unknown. There, not in knowledge as such, lies his excellence.

Even more than the scholar, the statesman seems to be bound by a chain of cause and effect, subject to pressures which leave little room for the flight of intuition. Yet, every statesman of historical stature has made decisions that were not merely the aggregate of previous observations and deliberations but based on intelligent guesses within the undeterminateness of great historical moments. President Kennedy's resolve about the Russian missiles in Cuba was of that nature.

The subtle kinship between the mind of the great statesman and the artistic-intuitive type explains also the fact that great political leaders are often impressive speakers and also writers of high achievement; Caesar, Napoleon, Bismarck, Churchill, and Lincoln come to mind. Certainly, the charisma of political leadership, as of any kind of leadership, arises out of a convergence of many qualities, but the aesthetic and imaginative qualities must be among them. They also help to create the fascination that surrounds great leaders—the "charisma."

Intuition is sometimes equated with inspiration. There is, however, a difference. The intuitive mind works as an active agent, whereas inspiration connotes a receptive quality. According to myth, the Bible was the work of inspired minds. They were receptacles and felt themselves to be so. They would have refused to be called inventors. Nevertheless, there is a subtle kinship between intuition and inspiration. It needs a degree of intuition to discover the sources of inspiration. The dull mind is blind to them.

One serious objection could be made against the preceding emphasis on imagination and intuition as conditions of creativeness. Granting that they have guided unusual minds into new fields of knowledge, they have also led individuals and whole societies into the snares of self-deception and delusions of grandeur. People of some experience can generally distinguish the lunatic would-be savior of mankind from the true opener of new paths of wisdom. Nevertheless, false prophets have found devoted followers, especially among materially and spiritually starving fellow men. The history of religion is replete with sham apostles, and where religion lost its power, nationalist and racial fanaticisms took its place. Not only in desperate Germany but also in more fortunate countries Hitler was admired as the messenger of Aryan destiny and the source of unfailing intuition.[19] Indeed, it would be easy for a historian to prove how, through the course of time exploiters have thrived on the desire of many men to flee from reason back to the womb.

What, then, is the difference between the mere vagaries of imagination and productive intuition? We have already spoken of a built-in logic in every creative act. Now we have to go

19. See E. Seillière, *Mysticisme et domination. Essais de critique impérialiste* (Paris: Bibliothèque de philosophie contemporaine, 1913).

one step further, the sixth one. The difference between the false and the authentic genius lies in a *special relation to reality, or a responsibility to truth.* Whereas the false prophet believes himself to be the incarnation of truth, the creative man is the devoted seeker. Whereas the former is incapable of self-correction and is therefore the propagandist of fanaticism, the latter suffers from a deep sense of incompleteness. The former represents the closed, the latter the ever open mind. He will gratefully enjoy the moment when the work he has planned is completed, whether it be a symphony finished, a mathematical problem solved, or a political action successfully performed. Without the hope and delight of certainty there would be no seeking. But it is probably only in the field of art and of mathematics that one can speak of a work that is so round and so whole and true that little or nothing can be changed. Every other human creation has in itself the germ and chance for both the better and the worse.

Seeking the truth, either by means of action or of reason, or by means of aesthetic comprehension, is an arduous exercise which most people like to avoid. But if it leads eventually to the desired result, then there emerges a sense of intimacy with kindred minds working even in different areas of thought. This is the finest delight of the educated person.

In the language of the religious mystic, man then becomes aware of his unity with the center of Being in which we all are united. He may call it "God." In secular language, he understands somewhat better the order of things and thus, being less ignorant than before, feels richer and freer. Even with the risk of persecution he cannot help but tell his fellow men what he has found. In all humility, he feels under the shadows of the great representatives of intellectual depth and progress, a Socrates, a Michael Servetus, a Giordano Bruno, a Spinoza, and all those whom mankind admires as leaders on the path of civilization.

Here we enter the seventh and last point of our discussion of creativity, namely, *involvement or commitment.* The scientist who has solved a new problem enjoys a sense of achievement, or of freedom from former uncertainty. But at the same time, his involvement deepens. He feels compelled to go on. It is the mark of the dilettante that, during intervals between his work, he can completely forget about it or drop it if it turns out to be arduous. It has not become a part of his being; it has no hold on him because he has no hold on it.

Thus, a paradox appears. The freer the creative person feels because he has overcome his former limitations, the more he becomes the servant of a perhaps ever distant goal. There develops, as it were, a lasting mutual loyalty between person and purpose. In more than twenty dialogues Plato tried to clarify the relation of man to himself, to his fellow men, and to the universe, hiding his name behind that of his master Socrates. With heroic patience, Aristotle designed the first intellectual map that oriented generation after generation on their journey toward truth. Newton went from experiment to experiment in the attempt to understand the *arcana dei* hidden in nature, and Goethe finished as an old man the *Faust* which from his youth had accompanied him throughout his life. Creative involvement could be compared to a great love with all its contradictions: won with difficulty, yet in a spirit of exaltation; sometimes lost in disappointment, yet always reconquered; a never ending concern and therefore a never ending source of self-development.

The academic professions believe too easily that the mere occupation with human subjects or with the laws of society and nature produces per se a more humane, lawful, and committed person. One could, of course, point to the lower rate of criminality among the educated. But that is due partly to hereditary factors; to a generally more protected upbringing; to a more sheltered life which guarantees a decent existence, even with modest income; and to a relatively high intelligence which generally helps a person see that his self-interest is best guarded when he follows the rules of decency. But in periods of stress, political and otherwise, the teaching profession has fallen disappointingly short of the ideals proclaimed in times of security. Forgotten were the great authors whose books were nicely arranged, often unread, on the bookshelves. The most uncreative attitude, cynicism, is the besetting sin of the intellectual. But the creative mind feels the ethos of his work. He wants to share with society the gift he has received from nature. He must not only be what he is; he must also give what he has.

Here is the ever increasing challenge to schools. Modern technology demands abstract knowledge and therefore a prolonged education. Will such higher education, which up to the nineteenth century was given only to about 5 percent and is now the privilege of about 30 percent of the school population of the United States, provide merely a "neutral" or a "useful" information, or will it become an integrated and vital element in the cultural future of humanity? If we fail, the modern extension of the school age will produce the kind of disaster that always results from irresponsible sophistication and semi-intellectuality. If, on the other hand, we succeed in combining more learning with more commitment, then Eve, the mother of curiosity, and Prometheus, the bringer of fire, will not regret that they stole the arts of knowledge and industry from the domain of jealous gods.

Why should a discussion of education in a modern social democracy include an analysis of the exceptional mind? Except in a few selective institutions, teachers have to adjust their demands to the large average with half of the class just dragging behind. Even under the most modest requirements, 40 percent [20] of the pupils leave high school after the tenth grade. A quick perusal of leading newspapers and journals suffices to inform us about the strains and trials of public education. At the White House Conference on Education in 1965 the participants agreed that too many teachers were satisfied with minimum results and careless about the floods of failure, and that school administrators, truly described as a timid lot, knew little about their communities and disposed all too quickly of difficult social cases by relegating them to welfare departments. Students of limited talent are—so we hear—forced out of the school because they are offered nothing that interests them. They are the victims of grade systems, of antiquated methods, and of incompetent

20. See Solomon Lichter, *The Drop-outs* (New York: Free Press, 1963), Preface.

teachers. Francis Keppel, former U.S. commissioner of education, declared that we "are still staffing classrooms with poorly paid and untrained personnel" and that "recruitment policies settle for mediocrity and discriminate against teachers of particular races and religions." According to Mr. Keppel, more than ten million children of poverty lack proper medical care and are frequently ill and not in school. Teen-age syphilis has grown by more than 200 percent since 1956, and most larger communities are fighting juvenile delinquency, which has doubled in ten years.

The increasing competition for entrance into nationally well-known colleges induces an increasing number of students to cheat, sometimes with the connivance of their instructors. Psychologists doubt whether we can fill all the high-order jobs needed in our technological age with competent people, since IQs of at least 120, necessary for such positions, are above the intelligence of 90 percent of the population.

Finally, looking at the world at large, we are informed by the United Nations Food and Agriculture Organization and World Health Organization that "over 80 percent of the world's population does not receive sufficient daily protein, while some 60 percent verges on actual protein starvation." [21] Ten to 20 percent of the children of this group will be mentally and physically retarded. Under these circumstances, is the emphasis on a creative elite not an exercise in utopianism?

There are two reasons for this emphasis. First, those who do not dare aim at the top of the mountain will always remain on a level below their capacity. Millions underestimate their strength because they have never really tried it. Second, however great the qualitative differences, nature has not split those of high and those of low endowment into halves with a yawning chasm between them. They are all human beings with hearts and brains, diverse in their productivity but not in their essentiality, just as a Mozart and a simple music lover have something in common—or, if the materialist metaphor be permitted—a diesel engine works on the same principle whether it is large or

21. *New York Times*, December 24, 1965.

small. Furthermore, let us not forget that the common man may compensate for his intellectual shortcomings by greater strength in nonintellectual areas of human performance. Also there is a great chance for creativity or excellence. An intelligent carpenter would probably survive more easily on a lonely island than many a famous professor.

This faith in the essential identity of the human person is not merely a sentimental pedagogical humor; the survival of the best in modern civilization depends on it. It underlies our idea of justice, equality, democracy, and all the great historical declarations of human rights.

The qualities we have described as characteristic of the creative person—spontaneity, sensitivity, self-discipline, purposefulness, intuitiveness, truthfulness, and commitment—are potentially inherent also in the average man. He also participates in the total productivity of life, unless—unfortunately, it happens all too often—his initiative is crushed by forces beyond his control, perhaps even in early youth. The nurturing of talent takes more time and effort in the slow than in the quick and even then will lead only to modest results. Resignation is a part of teaching. But even the less intelligent child must have a chance to learn under teachers who show him their respect by making demands as high as possible within the limits of his mental power. Underrating a student is sometimes more disastrous than overrating one.

But there is also a cruelly realistic issue behind the obligation of a modern nation to educate both its potential elite and the immense number of average students. For it has never become as evident as today that each of the two groups depends on the other; if the link is broken, disaster knocks at the door.

No longer can we, as in earlier times, keep a considerable part of humanity in the cellar. We feel now more than ever the immorality of such a situation; also, we cannot afford the waste of potential talent. Furthermore, the poor have absorbed at least enough enlightenment to know that poverty does not result from divine dispensation but from human error. With all their weakness they have nevertheless become strong enough to organize themselves and to continue the process of self-help that began during the nineteenth century when the leaders of worker units called the exploited laborers to collective action. In Russia, where the intelligence and energy for such collectivist action was missing, the peasant remained virtually a slave until the Revolution of 1917. In some parts of the world, men are still treated like cattle.

One need only read the plays and stories of Maxim Gorky and compare his descriptions of the animallike life of the illiterate masses with the life of their children and grandchildren, who can read and write. Sooner or later the time must come when they will no longer permit a dictatorial government to keep them in mental cages. Someday they will use their knowledge as participants in man's search for creative freedom. Famous Russian poets and scientists address the world pleading for a greater degree of intellectual freedom within the Soviet Union and throughout other parts of the world, as did the physicist Andrei Sakharov in his document, "Thoughts on Progress, Peaceful Coexistence and Intellectual Freedom."[22]

Similar events will doubtless occur in Mao-Tse-tung's China. As long ago as in 1668, the great Moravian scholar and educator John Amos Comenius noted in his *Way of Light* (Via Lucis):[23]

> For there is inborn in human nature a love of liberty—
> for liberty man's mind was convinced that it was made
> —and this love can by no means be driven out; so that
> wherever and by whatever means it feels that it is
> hemmed in and impeded, it cannot but seek a way
> out and declare its own liberty.

(6) *The Lack of Philosophical Design.* There are two aspects that could prevent us from indulging in the optimistic mood expressed by Comenius. We may sometimes doubt whether an "inborn love of liberty" lives in the human race. Furthermore, even those of us who would like to take the risk of freedom,

22. Printed in the *New York Times*, July 22, 1968; not yet published in the Soviet Union.
23. *Way of Light*, trans. by E. T. Campagnac (Liverpool: University Press, 1939), p. 18.

cannot do so in the face of contradicting goals or insufficient alternatives.

When John Amos Comenius and his contemporaries made the first steps toward universal schooling, they intended not only to improve the methods of education; learning for them, as for John Milton, was a way of man to God. The more he progressed in learning, the more chance he would have of achieving universal peace, protected by a hierarchy of values that would teach him how to distinguish the important from the unimportant, in his personal life as well as with regard to the subjects that should be taught in school.

If schooling means the same thing as knowledge, then we should be satisfied. Even in mediocre schools pupils learn now more than Comenius could ever have dreamed of. In good schools they learn more than their grandfathers learned in schools of high reputation. What they miss in languages, they gain in the sciences. On the whole, also the modern teacher is better trained in pedagogy and child psychology than his predecessors, though in terms of scholarly preparation only a very few could compare with such teachers as those in the old European classical schools to whom we owe outstanding books and monographs on humanistic topics.

But with all our progress in certain fields, we have lost what Comenius had—an over-all purpose that would place education in a great human scheme, or a philosophy of education within a cosmic philosophy of humanity. We have become manipulators whose research and experiments lead more and more to fragmentation. As a result, the schools of today, from the beginning grades to the university, have built up an administrative bureaucracy far greater than has ever existed anywhere. But how can even the most refined theories of motivation motivate a pupil who has to learn such and such quantities of "subject matter," not because it enriches him, but because he needs it for earning the number of credits necessary for examinations, which in turn are required for earning a living. Instinctively, the student knows that he is moved around like a chessman on the board of human existence.

Much of what most public schools afford today in terms of

an interpretation of man's life is a spineless eclecticism, mixing colorless residues from the Christian tradition with dehydrated pieces of humanism and naturalistic pragmatism. As a result, the schools cannot give the teachers a sense of commitment that would inspire their pupils, namely, the commitment for the unity of mankind. For this needs a practical idealism that can be found only at a few places. But should we blame the schools for the absence of courageous transcendence that is lacking in our whole society?

(7) *The Antibiological Quality of Modern Education.* Besides the lack of philosophical design, there exists a further over-all cause of the unrest in modern education. It is *antibiological* in extreme. It was not so a hundred years ago when not even 3 percent of the population of the Western nations were sitting for more than eight or ten years on school benches. These young men were for the most part proud of what they considered a privilege; they were gifted and personally involved in their learning; and most of them had comfortable homes in a natural environment which compensated for the dirt in dormitories and classrooms. Cleanliness was difficult for our ancestors anyhow.

With 30 percent of our young men and women attending schools of advanced education, one wonders about the mentality and motivation of many of them. One may take a walk around the squares and streets in the neighborhood of large universities. The students crowding the sidewalks are in the prime of both their sexual and intellectual capacity. They are desirous of action (except the nonsensical type enforced upon them by the military). When their ancestors were as old as they, they were apprenticed to a craftsman. Sometimes they were roughly treated, but they learned to forge an iron bar or to build a cabinet. Today, automatic machinery does it much quicker. One of the greatest benefits in the life of youth of earlier times, the institution of apprenticeship, is almost lost. Our young men sailed the seven seas or went on horseback across the continent to stake out a piece of land. At present, they live, often three or four of them, in apartments or dormitories with windows from which one looks on dreary streets or into other dusty windows.

There are alternatives to all this bookishness, an interaction between theory and paid practical work as practiced in some colleges. Some observers maintain that more could be done if the trade unions, zealously guarding the rights of their members, were more cooperative. One sometimes wonders whether they belong to the progressive or the reactionary side of our democratic society. Certainly, the social idealism that inspired their leaders in the nineteenth century has been drowned in the mentality of competitive capitalism and self-centered bureaucracy. The heroic time of union labor is gone.

(8) *The Professorial Empire.* More and more critical students, especially in the humanities, rightly suspect that many teachers are motivated, not by a profound urge for knowledge, but by the desire to preserve or expand their vested interests. Thus, they force on their students a number of courses which they need neither for their personal enrichment and maturity nor for their professional life, while they rob them of the chances for satisfying their curiosity in other areas of human engagement. More than one "paper empire" has been built upon the shaky foundations of "required courses."

Certainly, one should not measure the work of universities with the efficiency principles of industry. However, sometimes one might be inclined to apply to higher education the postulate that the amount of work should be commensurate with the product. How long would a business corporation survive if there were so little relation between labor and output as in our colleges and universities? Can the nation afford the colossal waste? Why, for example, must a prospective high school teacher of English take courses along the whole scale from Beowulf to modern literary criticism (frequently taught by teachers who have never written anything)? Should he not be able to interpret a piece of literature without having had a course on it? In addition, such a student has to attend education courses which often elucidate the obvious and elaborate on merely practical matters instead of helping him to understand education as a great cultural enterprise related to almost every important concern of mankind. Will such a teacher be better prepared to project himself into the excitement of a poet and convey some of it to his students?

Here is one of the explanations why we have relatively few scientists among rioting students. They are confronted with a closely interacting order of subjects, each of them as important for the whole as any other. Unfortunately, their requirements are often so exacting that they have no time left for interests in the larger concerns of mankind. Thus, something can be said for a certain disorderliness in the humanities. It may seem to be a waste of time, but it gives the critical student in this field room to contemplate and to reflect on the heights and abysses, the joys and sorrows, and the successes and failures of humanity. Thus he may become more sensitive to the troubles of our own time than many of his science-minded fellow students. On this sensitiveness and its transformation into socially productive action depends the future of the human race.

Hence, just as in our primary and secondary schools we need a new understanding of what it means to become a fully mature and reflective human being, so we need also in our institutions of higher education a radical self-examination of the role of the humanities, or the so-called liberal arts. To what degree do they still liberalize a young person's mind for absorbing and developing further the values which make a civilized community out of a mere collection of people? Certainly, they no longer occupy the central place in higher education they once held. For this their devotees blame the natural sciences, looking with envy at the financial support which the latter receive as the result of their growing influence on the life of modern man.

Actually, it needs only a quick historical examination of the catalogues of universities to discover that during the past decades the humanities have expanded more than at any other period, though they have lagged behind the natural sciences, the growth of which has been exceeded by the faculties of medicine, engineering, business administration, the social sciences, education, and journalism. This expansion of applied fields of learning and research demonstrates that we can no longer have a university of pure and disinterested scholarship, as imagined by Abraham Flexner in his book, *Universities, American, English, German*,[24] originally published in 1930. This book should still be read, for it is one of the best historical studies in the field of comparative education. Nevertheless, if our universities refused to respond in a systematic fashion, to the many practical questions which people such as businessmen and farmers expect to be answered, they would demand separate institutes. And these institutes would probably be of minor quality.

However, there is something highly contemporary in Flexner's book. It is the warning against the growth of trivialities hiding behind the shield of scholarship. Our liberal arts departments often have got stuck in pedantic philology, in historicism, in skeptical reflections on the troubles of the time, without offering any solutions, and in proving that a great action, after all, was not as great as had been thought, but was simply the result of egotistic motives. Such education, especially when furnished by mediocre minds, may destroy more in human substance than it builds. Rarely appears before the mind of the disenchanted student the colorful, yet somehow unified, landscape of human history, as the educated man saw it in earlier times. Rather, he is confronted by hundreds of little intellectual bailiwicks with high fences around small gardens.

Furthermore, the humanities apply now more and more the methods of exact science, including the computer, to works of literature. This is perfectly legitimate in certain areas of philological research, in such fields as linguistics, for example. But why blame the exact sciences for lack of human passion (of which, when deeply understood, they do not suffer at all) if one adopts more and more of their statistical and experimental methods even to subjects the real meaning of which will be forever inaccessible to statistical methods. The humanities should use any method that helps man to understand himself, but ultimately their true task is valuing and individualizing.

But one should not blame the humanities too severely for their state of uncertainty, for this state is a reflection of our whole culture, which no longer believes in anything ultimate

24. New edition, with an Introduction by Robert Ulich (New York: Teachers College Press [Columbia University], 1967).

and therefore has lost the sense of what is important and what is unimportant, in the areas of knowledge as well as in life as a whole.[25] Nevertheless, the humanities should be a bulwark against the flattering tendencies of our time. They should not be carried away by them.

In a real sense, we learn through inspiration and example, through motivation, through trial and error and self-examination, and, although mostly unconsciously, through the intellectual and moral atmosphere we inhale. For the continual creation and re-creation of this atmosphere the humanities are partly responsible. If they are pedantic and cheerless, even the richest and most modern program will be ethically ineffectual. Some living poetry (not merely literature) must occasionally break through the routine of the day. And the children, though enjoying their vacation, must also like to return to school.

ing in the United States. (New York: Harcourt, Brace, 1959), and W.
25. See Howard Mumford Jones, *One Great Society; Humane Learn-*David Maxwell, "A Methodolical Hypothesis for the Plight of the Humanities," *AAUP Bulletin* (March, 1968).

EPILOGUE

1. POLITICS AND THE ECONOMY

Life has often, and rightly, been described as a continuous conflict between polarities. Never was this truer than now. On the political and economic scene, we no longer possess the self-assurance and sense of white superiority characteristic of the bourgeois era. Rather we are now aware of the interdependence and the universality of the human race. London, Paris, Berlin, and Leningrad (Saint Petersburg) are no longer the capitals of the world, the orders of which the rest of mankind was expected to obey. These capitals had one thing in common. They were possessed by the deceptive sense of European superiority which even their nationalist rivalry, so they thought, would not destroy. It is difficult to believe today that less than a century lies between our decade and the diplomatic correspondences of King Edward VII, President Poincaré, Kaiser Wilhelm II, and Czar Nicholas II.

As early as in 1904, when the Japanese defeated Russia, far-sighted Europeans foresaw traumatic changes in the political constellation of the twentieth century. But it was World War I, that caused the avalanche of change and violence to roll over the seemingly secure pastures of Western civilization. After the end of the conflict the Russian autocracy no longer existed, the German and Austrian monarchies had collapsed. Too long would be the list of the changes in smaller countries such as Spain, Portugal, the Balkans, and the unfortunate lands right between the eastern German and the Russian borders. Finally, 1968 marked the end of the British Empire, the fleet of which had for centuries controlled the oceans. Some colonies still exist, though precariously. Colonialism as a world phenomenon, however, belongs to the past.

Certainly, not only mutual fear and the threat of nuclear war but also growing understanding of the causes and their differences have brought about some uneasy rapprochement between the two great powers, Soviet Russia and the United States. They already feel the menace of the giant China, now torn by inner strife but because of the ingenuity of its ancient people well capable of achieving the intellectual, technical, and military advances that have raised the Western nations and Russia to their present privileged position. Once fully equipped, the Chinese, who then may constitute one-fourth of the world's population, will attempt to lure to their side nations that may still live in jungles and huts but are nevertheless extremely important allies. For, as the English, French, and Americans have experienced, due to geographical advantages combined with the primitiveness of their living, these nations cannot be defeated by modern armies unless they are totally annihilated.

Is the Western world prepared to meet the political challenge of the future? Badly, we must confess, if we observe the ignorance and indifference of the large masses with regard to everything that transcends their immediate interests. Even many statesmen still live in the shadow of old isms—nationalism, capitalism, communism and anticommunism, as if there were nothing in between. The few with wider horizons are caught in a dilemma. Either they use the old hoary vocabulary (though they no longer believe in it) in order to assure their reelection by businessmen, veterans, trade unions, and other mass-minded organizations, or their followership will be too small to assure them of victory. The few who, like Senator Eugene McCarthy, dare push through the curtain of prejudice, will be opposed by their own party and may lose whatever chance to speak to the nation's youth, which is waiting for guidance. Only a few Fulbrights can be found throughout the world.

No doubt, the youth of all nations would fight as bravely as their ancestors if they had reason to believe they were attacked by an aggressor. Nothing closes a group more than danger brought about by a common enemy. But there can also be no doubt that today's young no longer identify themselves almost automatically with their nation and its symbols. They have become skeptical, if not cynical, about the ways the world is governed. Underneath the cold war, called peace, the fires of the hot war are constantly smoldering. Young people have no illusions about the glory of war because it has turned into mass murder. Modern warfare has rendered almost obsolete the international Red Cross laws of Geneva concerning the separation of soldiers and the civilian population. In any case, these laws did not exist but for a few decades of the nineteenth century; they were never applied to the natives of foreign continents. In colonial wars, the laws of the jungle were still accepted. They still reign in Vietnam; but, at least, more and more Americans have a bad conscience about it. The courts have to grapple with the question whether the burning of draft cards has to be considered conspiracy or not.

In contrast with England, in this country the word "politician" has acquired a dubious connotation because it smells of lobbies, bribery, and corruption, not as much as in the Balkans of earlier times or as in some parts of South America and Asia today, but badly enough. Despite all changes on the political scene nationalism persists. The old nations still bask in the glory of the past and, at the same time, are afraid that without vigilance they may fall back in the struggle for political and economic influence. On the other side, the developing nations feel that they will not be considered equals by the great powers unless they establish their national identity. They waver between feelings of inferiority and of exaggerated pride. Many realms are in the same or even more chaotic situation that Germany and Italy were in before their unification in the nineteenth century, or that France was in before the period of absolutism. Even during the French Revolution "federalism," or the desire of certain provinces to break off from Paris, was a threat to the nation's continuity.

Ireland went through its war of independence in the first half of this century but is still smarting under its division; the inner unity of Belgium is threatened by its bilingualism. De Gaulle tried to exploit the existence of the French language in

Canada, though farmers in Quebec and in the Dordogne no longer understand each other, and there are other examples of which one might be inclined to speak of as a kind of recidivism of almost buried hatreds. In England old nationalist resentments are increasing. The claim of the Scottish party for a separate constitution, a claim that was ridiculed fifty years ago, may sooner or later become a reality, and a number of Welsh patriots no longer consider it an honor that the English crown prince traditionally bears the title Prince of Wales. It would be easy to extend the number of illustrations, from the areas of communism where the satellites are becoming increasingly restless, to Africa and Asia.

Nevertheless, in spite of all hostility and jealousy, no power can extricate itself from the international scene without inviting catastrophe. In his 1968 New Year's Eve address, De Gaulle revived the almost forgotten French oratory of *gloire* to the degree of insanity. Nevertheless, he felt obliged to make some generous concessions to the existence of other nations. He described France as "a great people on the march" and as an "infallible beacon of the world," but he asserted that the goal of French world leadership he was seeking was at the same time "in the interest of mankind." [1] Certainly, double morality and military parades still characterize our political life, but let us believe that our statesmen, like most mammals of a high order, engage in the show of might in the hope they will sufficiently frighten the enemy so that battle can be avoided. The light of world consciousness is gradually permeating the dark woods of isolationism and will make it a bit easier for humanity to chart its future intelligently.

         ✿   ✿   ✿

When we turn our eyes to the *economic* situation, we meet the same paradox we find in the political realm. On the one hand, riches have accumulated, and the governments present budgets beyond the wildest imagination of earlier times. When

1. *Washington Post,* January 1, 1968.

President Lyndon Johnson prophesied the advent of the "Great Society," the means for urgent social reforms were available. But almost one half of the taxpayers' money goes for humanly unproductive purposes such as armament and wasteful bureaucracies. The so-called affluent society is a reality and a myth at the same time. It is a reality in that in advanced countries even a modest household is today equipped with heat and light, a refrigerator, a washing machine, a radio and a television set—beyond the dreams of a pre-world war citizen. It is a myth in that inflation, speculation, and the manipulations by big industrial companies are a continuous threat to a family's security. Furthermore, the increase of demands, caused by barrages of advertising and the desire for social prestige, often exceeds a family's resources and quickly turns every diminution of income, every prolonged sickness, and the helplessness of old age into disaster. In spite of public education, the expenses for professional preparation grow from year to year. For all these reasons, more and more people depend on state aid. Hence they live in a kind of bondage to the state which may look like patriotism but is actually a collective insecurity complex.

Nevertheless, the economically advanced countries have outgrown the era when the owners of capital and machines could freely exploit the have nots. The old Marxian concept of the proletariat has disappeared as a politico-economic concept, except in the writings of Russian authors against the injustices of the capitalist system. Although we still have slums and hopelessness in our midst, at least we try to correct the worst evils and wish to contribute to the emergence of a just society.

How does the economic situation look on the international scene? The economic gap between the advanced and the underdeveloped countries of the world appears to be as wide if not wider than the political. The task of the various world organizations which want to bring the rich and the poor nations closer to each other is an enormous one. The execution of the many economic measures planned since World War II appears to be far more complex than anticipated. Even in the United States, as we saw, aid to poor families or to slums is of little avail unless it serves as an energizing element by creating work, hope, initiative, and the desire for self-help. But if the environment constantly defeats human endeavor; the result is a sense of frustration that in turn defeats future planning. This is exactly what threatens the relation between the rich and the poor nations. Not only will the rich produce more and more with greater speed than the less developed countries, their chemists will invent ever new synthetic processes that will enable them to become independent of goods previously imported from the natural riches of Asia, Africa, and South America.

According to a lecture which the Harvard biologist Roger Revelle gave at the annual meeting of the American Association for the Advancement of Science (December 28, 1967), the poor countries will profit less from the wonders of the modern scientific revolution than the ghetto dwellers in our cities. The advent of synthetic rubber has caused a 50 percent decline in natural rubber production; the fabrication of synthetic fiber has more than doubled in the richer countries and has created havoc among the old cotton growers. We will have more and more durable synthetic leather and sooner or later also synthetic tea, coffee, and cocoa. At the same time, the rich nations will constantly drain precious manpower from those lands which are most in need of inventive genius. Some experts also predict that sooner or later large forests will be a liability rather than an asset to their owners, as wood becomes increasingly replaced by plastics. However, even if forests become a financial liability to the owner, the need for areas of plant life to produce oxygen is an absolute requirement of man's survival.

Of course, grand-scale relief will retain its value after the occurrence of natural catastrophes such as earthquakes or bad harvests. And as everywhere else, money will still mean power; but still greater power will be the knowledge of how to use it. Without the latter, the influx of money may even be a curse, as the history of Spain after the establishment of its colonies unmistakably shows. But how can our technical concepts of productivity be injected into groups that are suddenly awakened by the roar of airplanes and helicopters from thousands of years of slumber in the arms of nature—a nature not always kind, but nevertheless a familiar habitat? Man is the most adaptable creature on earth, but the jump from primitive agriculture and shamanism to modern industry and cybernetics is almost beyond human power to comprehend.

Therefore it is one of the most dangerous illusions—one with which the United States is especially affected—to believe that the large number of the newly founded nations will be able to change within a lifetime their familiar forms of social organization into some form of democracy. For democracy is not only a political and economic institution; it is also a cultural phenomenon. Without the latter, a society becomes a collective, efficiently engineered, but containing only the outward forms of democracy.

That leads us back to the political situation. Indeed, Western democracies no longer impress observers from other parts of the world, whether, like the Indian or other Asian nations, they still root precariously in cultures older than that of the West and consider it to be a sort of agglomeration of rich parvenus, or whether, like some African nations, they first glide into a sort of cultural no-man's-land before they find themselves again—if they ever will find themselves. However, their leaders, many of them graduates from European and American universities, are not fools. They know that they have to break their own trail toward salvation. On their way toward selfhood they may use totalitarian as well as democratic forms of administration. But they have learned from bitter experience that there is an ocean of difference between using the help of a great power and becoming its satellite. Either they will decay, or, once fortified against the lure of propaganda and imported money, they will adopt the best of either side to their own indigenous needs and, perhaps, develop completely new forms of communal living. In the emergence of new political organizations on the part of nations which hitherto were—and partly still are—instruments of imperialist powers lies one of the hopes of the future.

2. RELIGION AND HUMANISM

The same polarity between progress and failure, hope and frustration, observed in the political and economic fields will be noted in religion and humanism.

On the one hand, the high walls that have divided the Christian denominations from each other and from the world at large are gradually crumbling. The knots of dogma are being untied, with clergymen leading in the process. And while high ecclesiastical dignitaries pay polite visits to each other, their subordinates engage in discussions and actions which twenty years ago would have been considered heretical if not outrageous. No longer is a Catholic priest regarded, nor does he regard himself, as supernaturally shielded from the ordinary man's desire for love, wife, and family. Many priests defend birth control. In the United States every bishop needs an adviser as to what to do with his erring or wavering priests. In 1969, the bishop of Saint Paul–Minneapolis, resigned. He also got married.

Throughout the world, the sense of social responsibility invades the quiet precincts of the devoted life. Since 1967 monks and nuns, frustrated by their vain attempts to ameliorate the lot of the poor Indians of Guatemala, have cooperated with the Communist underground. In Spain, anti-Franco priests meet secretly with the workers. New forces of religious activism and socialism emerge also in Protestantism. The ecumenical spirit prevails.

On the other hand, in the life of the mind just as in the human heart there seems to be a rhythm between expansion and contraction. Conservative Catholics complain that their church is becoming more and more Protestant; and conservative Protestants are afraid of losing their individualistic tradition in the general spirit of reconciliation and ritualism.

Religious obscurantism still holds its place against enlightenment. In our daily newspapers the Knights of Columbus advertise the medieval doctrines of salvation. Some wealthy Protestants prefer the faith healer to the physician until it is too late. On the lowest level of some sort of awareness of man's dependence on higher forces, millions of American citizens spend billions for the divination of palm readers and crystal gazers. Many leading newspapers carry a column on astrology, often of an incredible insipidity. In troubled Ireland of 1971, only barbed wires erected by armed soldiers could separate the fighting Catholics and Protestants. Nevertheless, religious wars, such as were waged in earlier centuries, belong to the past. Unfortunately, the desolation they left in the souls of men who lust for the fires of hatred has been filled by still more cruel nationalist wars. If one investigates the psychology of these wars, one is amazed at the frequent recurrence of religious motives. We have not yet outgrown the medieval mixture of religion and politics. Subliminal, and exactly for this reason highly dangerous, religious prejudices still determine relations among peoples. The ordinary Western view of communism is not only economically, but also religiously, prompted. Without the missionaries in East Asia and the powers behind them, our relation to China and Vietnam would be different. The catastrophic political decisions of former American Secretary of State John Foster Dulles cannot be explained without reference to the religious component in his makeup.

As has already been indicated in the sections on religion, it is impossible to say how many of us are still "Christians." Many regard themselves as such because they live, after all, in a so-called Christian culture; they support the churches for vague moral reasons; and they believe that the soul needs some kind of cult, even though its substance might not stand the proof of the intellect. They obey the desire that lives in every human soul: they want to belong, just as millions of people remain in families or communities which they do not like, merely because they are afraid of being alone. Therefore, they never think of more sincere alternatives.

Furthermore, since many parents are more anxious about their children than about themselves, they send them, at considerable expense, to private denominational schools with the hope that there they might receive a firmer direction for their future than in a secular environment. Will they?

Indeed, at least in the United States, impartial observers tend to believe that children who attend Christian or Jewish schools are less prone to the lure of drugs, sex, alcohol, and smoking than those who attend religiously noncommitted schools. But the same observers also agree that too many variables are involved to allow large generalizations, such as the cultural tradition of the family, its financial background, its motivation, and even regional factors relevant to it.

Young women anchored in some religious faith seem to remain more careful in the choice of sexual partners than the majority of their contemporaries. Apparently, religious modes of education, if understandingly applied and voluntarily accepted, preserve their effect on a person's behavior even if they have sunk from the level of concrete belief into the subconscious. They form an undercurrent that influences surface behavior.

But though different answers may be given to the problem of religious education, it is certain that at least in urban regions few churchgoers share the dogmatic faith of their ancestors. In spite of the warnings of the Vatican, the mass is interpreted symbolically by more and more Catholics; and for Protestant ministers the Eucharist, once the subject of bloody fights with their Catholic brethren, is today a matter of embarrassment.

Thus the problem arises: what is the future of Christianity? Religiously speaking, the majority of Western men live in a tradition that no longer exists, except that it stops them from risking constructive spiritual novelty. Here is the function of a new humanism. Freed from the old antimetaphysical rationalism and materialism, but accepting the ultimate mysteriousness of all being, it will be open to both the most radical scientific inquiry as well as to the language and emotional depth of religious symbolism.

Most people with an advanced education, if thinking deeply about themselves, would have to profess that they are humanists in that they base their thinking about man's role in the universe on rational premises and no longer on transcendental and mythical revelations. Only a free and constantly developing humanism can provide that synthesis between physics and metaphysics, science and religion, and empiricism and intuition which every culture needs in order to be complete.

3. EDUCATION

With our political and cultural life in the claws of the conflict between progress and retardation, it would be astonishing if education were an exception. Indeed, it appears to be not merely the mirror of the troubles of modern society but even a source of them. The reason is that, pragmatically speaking, more than ever individuals as well as whole nations realize that their future depends on their capacity to compete with their fellow men and with other countries in a brutal struggle for survival. Stagnation is the worst prospect we can think of.

But deeper motives are also working behind the present emphasis on education. They stem from the polarity between the continuous accumulation of theoretical and technical knowledge on the one hand, and human thought and conduct on the other. Of knowledge, we have an abundance. At the end of this century, when our present students will be at the peak of their careers and will have to carry the main responsibilities of social life, they will live in environment highly different from ours. They will use more effective machines for production and for transportation, the latter being just as important in the change of civilizations as the former. Some will live in underwater and underground houses. They may employ robots for domestic and industrial services. They may control the weather. More and more successfully they will transplant human organs and replace a damaged heart, lung, or kidney by an artificial one. They will create life in test tubes and determine the sex of unborn children. They will land on distant planets. Worldwide live television transmission will make neighbors out of antipodes. More and more they will feel not only that they are the inhabitants of the whole earth but of a cosmos of ever widening dimensions.

All this knowledge will largely be dispersed through the population by the schools. But when man can create man artificially while he can destroy all mankind by war, and when leisure time will be so extended that people do not know what to do with it, and when governments may try to use secret chemical means to reinforce the power of the instruments of communication and thus to dehumanize the minds of men— what kind of life will it be in such a situation of worldwide technical knowledge administered by unreliable forces? But let us not dwell on the worst that man could do to man.

It is a historical fact that the more uncertain man is about his future, the more he will shift the burden of responsibility to the schools. Will they be able to live up to his expectations?

When trying to answer the question, one becomes, first of all, aware of the gap between educational theory and educational practice in an age of transition. We just begin to ask in a scholarly and systematic fashion questions like these. On what factors does success or failure in high schools and schools of higher education depend? An unfortunate family environment, poverty, and the lack of vocabulary and of stimulating conversation are severe handicaps even to the potentially highly talented student.

How can we overcome social prejudices in schools the teachers of which have inherited these prejudices and consequently tend to transfer them to their pupils? Even more than the teachers, the parents lay value on preserving the status quo, though it is perilous to the future of their children when they force them to live with outmoded standards in a society in need of men of initiative.

The fervent discussion about the most appropriate size of a classroom is mostly based on guesses and generalizations. It may be sixteen to twenty or twenty-five to thirty, but it may also be two or one hundred. It all depends on the teacher, the subject, and the cooperation of the students. Furthermore, what constitutes achievement, and to what degree is it satisfactorily measured by our system of tests and examinations? It has been demonstrated again and again that various teachers grade differently the same essay, even the same mathematical assignment.

Some youth mature early; others, late. Some of the most creative men were mediocre students. Why? And why do so many of us have the feeling that the spontaneous creativity of

children declines at the age of twelve and often gives room
to lethargy which then turns into adolescent rebellion? Is this
an inevitable process of "acculturation" ("breaking in" might be
a better term), or can the spark of childhood be preserved?

Finally, two questions, which sound "undemocratic" to the
idealistic American educator who considers length of training
almost as a guarantee of professional satisfaction and efficiency.
Can a person be overschooled for his future vocation? Will an
extended theoretical preparation that inevitably arouses special
expectations be the right one for a man who day after day has
to read meters or make his monotonous rounds in a park? In his
state of frustration he may easily forget his role as a guardian
of democracy and use his club when, once in his empty life, he
sees a chance for greatness. Let us remember, that the vanguard
of Hitler's brownshirts was largely recruited from dissatisfied
university students who could find no adequate employment
during the depression of the 1930s.

The whole question of centralization and decentralization of
education is still based more on political than on rational considerations.[2] It will be a task of the future to establish rational
policy of education in order to answer the questions of the public
concerning the growing expenses and the unrest of the teachers
in our schools. Despite all differences, something could be
learned from the ways in which modern corporations combine
motivation, efficiency, and thrift.

But the main predicament of modern education results from
the fact that our schools, which account for one-fourth to one-
third of the life of well-educated man, deprive the human person
of the conditions of organic development. The secondary schools,
especially, are largely imitations of the past. In spite of much
change in content, they train one-sidedly the cognitive and verbal faculties, as if the latter were the only ones to form a character. Even a hundred years ago, when these schools prepared a

2. In connection with the points here discussed, see an article by
Hellmut Becker "Bildungsforschung und Bildungsplanung" (Educational
Research and Planning), in *Wirtschaft und Wisenschaft* (März, 1969).
Professor Becker is head of the Institut for Bildungsforschung in der Max
Planck Gesellschaft in Berlin.

minimal percentage of the nation's youth for the learned professions, the Danish bishop Grundtvig, father of the folk high
schools, who knew his people and its needs, called them "schools
for death," instead of "schools for life." Also Nietzsche, himself a
classical scholar, was convinced that they were a failure, even
with regard to understanding their mother tongue.

What we need is a radical, to repeat a radical, reorganization
of our school system. In addition to its classrooms and some
opportunities for sports, often used only by a minority, the
schools of the future should have workshops where every student
learns the rudiments of a craft and gardens and farms where he
learns to observe the growth of plants and animals; in other
words, schools where he learns that he is a part of nature and
not its master.[3]

Two objections will be made: first, the expenses; second, the
necessity of preparing youth for living in a technical world.

With regard to the expenses: provided the Vietnam war will
eventually end it will have devoured and will continue to devour
about three hundred and fifty *billion* dollars if we include the
costs in veteran benefits, medical expenses, and interest payments on federal debts. The costs for World War II will add up
to one trillion and fifty-seven billion dollars.[4] There was a reason
for the staggering expense of World War II; the free nations had
to fight the greatest threat to their existence. The question remains, however, whether Hitler could have come to power if
the Germans had had schools for life instead of "schools for
death." But there is no excuse for the insanity of the Vietnam
war, which has almost ruined our national economy, not to speak
of its effect on our conscience. What if even a fraction of the
$350 billion had been spent for a reform of our schools and for
internal and foreign aid!

The answer to the second objection, namely, that the school
reform here suggested is in contrast to our technological civilization, is simple. Just because of it! Unless we provide, during the

3. I have dealt with the design of such a school more elaborately in
my *Crisis and Hope in American Education* (New York: Atherton Press,
paperbound edition, 1967).

4. *Boston Globe,* June 29, 1969.

malleable age of man's life, a counterweight to the dangers of a mechanical society, the engineers will more and more determine the life and thought of humanity. In that engineered society we will not even enjoy its potential advantages because of the pollution of air, water, and food unless we bring up generations willing to fight these dangers. And that can be done only by means of schools which, supported by aroused communities, tell the young that they have to work with nature, not against it. For as we have experienced, when violated, nature hits back.

Unfortunately, we move here in a vicious circle which will be hard to break. How can we have new schools when we have parents with rigid minds and teachers whose finances forbid them to widen their judgment and imagination by visiting foreign countries?

But narrowness of mind is a predicament that confronts every reform. Except nature, almost everything that we enjoy today was once a dream. Only a few dared believe in it—those who were not afraid of being attacked or ridiculed. But they won to their side men of influence; they wrote books and thus guided the minds of more and more people toward their purposes, until the once suspected ideas became a topic of discussion and a part of the public will. It takes at least five decades until a novel idea becomes reality; sometimes it takes centuries. Especially in the field of education, the harvest ripens slowly.

Schools cannot perform miracles. Sometimes they have been miserably helpless against the demons of prejudice. But somehow they struggle out of the hole; they survive not only physically but in spirit as well. In spite of all compromises they have been forced to make in terms of content, at the basis of human learning there persist certain mental operations that transcend the boundaries of countries and point to the community of thinking men. When schools teach the sciences and mathematics, they teach the logic that inheres in them. Even the table of numbers, the crux of the first grader, illustrates the universality of the human approach to reality. It is the same for a child in Washington and in Peking. So let us not end this book in a negative key. It is through the conversations of a Socrates with the aristocratic youth of Athens, as well as through the patience (perhaps also the impatience) of an unknown village teacher, that Western man has built his culture. Western culture, with all its greatness, is now in danger because of its imbalance between operational knowledge and real wisdom, its self-alienation from nature, and also because of its arrogant isolation from the interests of other continents.

The Greeks conceived of education as a kind of statecraft. They were right. Kings, priests, interest groups, and republics have used education for good but also for evil aims. In the future, the tendency to exploit it will increase. While the influence of the churches will recede, or work more covertly than in the past, political groups, in close alliance with business, will increase their propaganda and try to enter into the classrooms of the schools and universities. And all the modern means of communication will be employed to direct the minds of the young.

Will the schools allow themselves to be pushed around like tools, or will they act as selective agencies and guardians of the spiritual inheritance of man? Will they help to create a society where men can listen to the best in themselves instead to selfish institutions? Only if they act wisely will they discover that we are all of the same flesh, or, in mythological terms, "children of God." They will listen to the call of history to re-create a vision which has inspired the minds of sages for almost three thousand years, namely, the unity of mankind as a part of the order of the universe.

INDEX

Adams, John Quincy, 37
Aeschylus, 33
Albert of Cologne, 34
Alexander II, Czar, 39
Alexander the Great, 43
Altitzer, Thomas, 135
Amery, Carl, 61
Aquinas, Thomas, 8, 34
Archimedes, 33
Aristotle, 8, 33ff., 146, 177
Arnold, Matthew, 5, 35, 146, 156

Bahai, 145
Bailey, James A., 121
Bakunin, 39
Balzac, Honoré, 7
Barnum, Phineas T., 121
Basile, Joseph, 126
Baudelaire, Charles, 76
Beach, Beatrice, 112
Becker, Hellmut, 200
Behrens, Peter, 45
Benoit, Emile, 111
Bent, Charles N., 135
Bergson, Henry, 69
Biber, Barbara, 168
Bismarck, 20, 28, 175
Bloch, Ernst, 92
Bonhoeffer, Dietrich, 133
"Bourgeois," 5
Browning, Elizabeth Barrett, 171
Buber, Martin, 69
Buisson, Ferdinand, 13

Bultman, Rudolf, 133, 136
Burhoe, Ralph Wendell, 136
Byron, Lord George, 35

Caesar, 175
Campagnac, E. T., 181
Camus, 77, 136
Carnot, Sadi, 39
Castro, 87
Cecil, Robert, 53
Churchill, 56, 175
Cicero, 147
Coleridge, Samuel, 35
Coles, Robert, 95
Comenius, John Amos, 181, 182
Comte, Auguste, 28
Confucius, 8
Copernicus, 34
Counts, George S., 22
Curie, Eve, 171
Cushing, Cardinal, 139

Dante, 174
Darwin, 15
Daschner, Karlheinz, 62
De Gaulle, 87, 190, 191
Deutsche Unitarier, 145
Dewey, John, 67ff., 79
Dickens, Charles, 7
Diderot, 11
Dilthey, Wilhelm, 69
Dreyfus, Captain, 13

Du Bois, E. B., 98
Dulles, John Foster, 196

Edward VII, 187
Edwards, Paul, 135
Einstein, Albert, 17
Elizabeth, Empress of Austria, 39
Emerson, Ralph Waldo, 145
Engels, 167
Erasmus, 171

Feuerbach, 15
Flaubert, Gustave, 7, 30
Flexner, Abraham, 186
Fox, Harvey, 135
France, Anatole, 7, 67, 100
Franklin, Benjamin, 37
Freud, Sigmund, 29, 32, 71, 141
Friedrich, Carl J., 10
Froebel, 39
Fulbright, 170, 189

Galbraith, John Kenneth, 125
Galileo, 34
Galsworthy, John, 7
Gandhi, 31
Garelik, Herbert M., 71
Gide, André, 33
Goebbels, Joseph, 54, 65
Goethe, 32, 35, 141, 155
Goldston, Eli, 120
Gorky, Maxim, 181
Gropius, Walter, 45
Grotius, Hugo, 10, 88
Grundtvig, 201

Haeckel, Ernst, 29
Hamilton, William, 135
Harrod, Roy F., 107
Heer, Friedrich, 62
Hegel, Friedrich Wilhelm, 10, 14
Heidegger, Martin, 75
Heine, Heinrich, 31
Hemingway, 77

Heraclitus, 8
Hirschauer, Gerd, 142
Hitler, 21, 24, 58ff., 79, 93, 96,
    105, 109, 115, 125, 175, 200
Hobbes, Thomas, 10, 84
Hoffman, Stanley, 83
Hölderlin, 35
Homer, 147
Hope, John, 98
Horace, 147
Hoselitz, Bert, 23, 170
Humbert I, King of Italy, 39
Humboldt, Wilhelm von, 146, 156
Hume, 11, 36
Husserl, Edmund, 75
Huxley, Aldous, 167

Jackson, President Andrew, 100
James, Henry, 7
James, William, 32, 68, 164
Jaspers, Karl, 74
Jaurès, Jean, 52
Jefferson, Thomas, 37, 118, 146
Jesus, 43, 137, 144
John XXIII, Pope, 137, 140ff.
Johnson, President Lyndon, 102,
    192
Jones, Howard Mumford, 187

Kafka, 77, 136
Kant, 36, 95
Kautsky, 54
Keller, Gottfried, 97
Kennedy, President John, 102, 168,
    174
Keppel, Francis, 179
Kessler, Harry Graf, 55
Keynes, John Maynard, 54
Kierkegaard, Soren, 29, 70ff., 144,
    145
King, Martin Luther, 167
Korsch, Karl, 92
Krapotkin, 39

Lansing, Robert, 53
Lao-Tzu, 166
Lascaux, 157
Le Corbusier, Charles, 45
Lenin, 23, 44, 54, 109
Lichter, Solomon, 176
Lincoln, Abraham, 130, 175
Locke, 36, 38
Lorenz, Konrad, 164
Lukacs, Georg, 92
Luther, 32, 43, 71, 144

Machiavelli, 84
Mann, Thomas, 7
Marcuse, Herbert, 116, 141
Mao-Tse-tung, 181
Marx, Karl, 5, 14ff., 39, 92, 167
Matteotti, Giacomo, 61
Maurras, Charles, 130
McCarthy, Eugene, 189
McCarthy, Joe, 93
McKinley, 39
Mies van der Rohe, 45
Mill, J. S., 23
Milton, John, 182
Mohammed, 95
Money, Ross, 170
Montaigne, 28, 32
Montesquieu, 11
Mozart, 179
Mussolini, 54, 61, 93
Myrdal, Gunnar, 89

Nader, Ralph, 126
Napoleon, 39, 175
Nash, Paul, 64
Newton, 177
Nicholas II, Czar, 188
Nietzsche, Friedrich, 29, 71ff., 141,
    167, 201
Nixon, President, 102, 115

Oedipus, 152
Orwell, George, 116, 167
Ottaviani, Cardinal, 138

Pascal, Blaise, 171
Paul VI, Pope, 99, 138, 140
Perla, Leo, 22
Pestalozzi, 39, 74, 79
Pike, James A., 133
Pius XII, Pope, 61
Plato, 8, 33, 44, 146, 159, 177
Plutarch, 147
Poincaré, President, 187
Pulley, Sande, 164
Pythagoras, 33

Quintilian, 35

Rathenau, 55
Razik, Teher, 170
Read, Sir Herbert, 167
Renan, Ernest, 28
Revelle, Roger, 193
Rilke, 136
Robinson, John, 133
Roosevelt, Franklin D., 37, 56
Rousseau, 36, 137
Ruskin, John, 19

Sadler, Michael Thomas, 20
Sartre, 136
Schiller, 35, 155, 171
Schleiermacher, 137
Schopenhauer, 30, 36
Semme, Bernard, 23
Shakespeare, 141
Shaull, Richard, 66
Shelley, Percy Bysshe, 36
Sibree, J., 10
Slichter, Sumner H., 59
Socrates, 202
Sophocles, 33
Spencer, Herbert, 11, 28, 32, 78
Spengler, Oswald, 79
Spinoza, 34, 84
Stalin, 56, 104, 115
Stanley, Henry Morton, 25
Steinmetz, Charles, 171

Strauss, David Friedrich, 28
Suarez, Francisco, 10

Tillich, Paul, 133, 136
Tinbergen, Jan, 108
Tocqueville, Alexis de, 7, 99
Trotzky, 55
Truman, President Harry, 102, 107

Ulich, Robert, 20, 40, 46, 74, 114, 136, 170, 186, 201
UNESCO, 86, 164

Vahanian, Gabriel, 135

Van Buren, Paul, 135
Veblen, Thorstein, 146
Verlaine, 76
Voltaire, 28, 36, 39

Washington, Booker T., 90, 98
Whitehead, Alfred North, 131
William II, 20, 187
Wilson, Edmund, 101
Wilson, President Woodrow, 52ff., 102
Wordsworth, William, 35

Zola, Emile, 7